A GUIDE TO
SHORE AND HARBOUR
FISHING

A GUIDE TO
SHORE AND HARBOUR
FISHING

FRANCIS H. BURGESS

With illustrations by the author

DAVID & CHARLES
NEWTON ABBOT LONDON
NORTH POMFRET (VT) VANCOUVER

ISBN 0 7153 7088X
Library of Congress Catalog Card Number 76-4371

Set in 11 on 13pt Baskerville
and printed in Great Britain
by Redwood Burn Limited
Trowbridge
for David & Charles (Publishers) Limited
Brunel House Newton Abbot Devon

Published in the United States of America
by David & Charles Inc.
North Pomfret Vermont 05053 USA

Published in Canada
by Douglas David & Charles Limited
1875 Welch Street North Vancouver BC

CONTENTS

INTRODUCTION

Sea-fishing is quite distinct from fresh-water fishing; the tackle used, the methods and conditions that apply, are all quite different and with little relevance to each other. One factor common to both, however, is the realisation that it is not always luck when someone reels fish in one after another, whilst his neighbour looks on catchless and enviously.

This book offers the beginner a progressive introduction to the sport of rod and line sea fishing, explaining in some detail what it is all about, how to set about it, and how, eventually, to become a competent and knowledgable angler.

This is followed by illustrated descriptions of most of the fish one may take in the harbours and around the shores of the British Isles, together with details of them and their habits. Though the scope of the book does not cover the many aspects of trips in larger boats out to deeper waters well away from beaches, referred to as sea-angling, there is of necessity an over-lapping fringe and so much relevant information, especially about the fish, has also been included.

Whilst nets, trots, long lines and suchlike can catch fish if it is quantity that is needed, no great skill is required nor sport obtained by such methods. Rod and line angling with suitable tackle can, on the other hand, provide a lifetime of good sport and one of the most fascinating of all hobbies.

Perseverance and patience will be needed to gain the special-ised knowledge and experience that make the successful sea angler, but the time spent and the frustrations often suffered will be well worth while, especially on the day when there comes that answer to the angler's prayer:

'Lord grant that I may catch a fish, So big, that even I,
When speaking of it afterwards, Will have no need to lie'.

F.H.B.

CHAPTER I

CHOOSING THE RIGHT EQUIPMENT

It would be wise to ponder well and learn all you can before embarking on the purchase of rods or tackle, and the first preliminary should be the preparation of a rough plan taking into account the types and methods of fishing you intend to undertake, and which are best suited to your locality.

If you intend to concentrate at first on pier or jetty fishing, you need not purchase a boat rod yet; if only small-boat trips are contemplated, then such things as casting rods and rod rests are unnecessary for the time being. With no pier or boat handy, or if your preference is for beach fishing, then, again, a different approach will be needed and the basic equipment varied accordingly.

Assimilate all the knowledge you can, and then prepare a list of primary essentials (rod, reel, line and weights) according to your needs, preference, and price; remembering that it is advisable, and most economical in the long run, to buy the best you can afford.

The various methods of fishing, suitable items of tackle for them, and other useful hints are explained later in some detail, and this information will help you to decide upon the equipment best suited to your particular requirements at the outset.

Later on, you will be able to augment your initial array of tackle by the acquisition of many smaller items such as swivels and buckles for making up traces, together with booms, floats, and suchlike. Then, when you have most of them, you can gradually build up your equipment with such larger items as rod rest, night lamp, gaff, waterproof clothing, soup flask, and any other accessories you may consider essential to your skill and enjoyment.

Before reaching the point where you will be ready for the 'Off', there are a few preliminary matters worth considering.

(1) If you have a local library handy, there is often a shelf full of books covering most aspects of fishing, and no doubt including the one you are most interested in.

(2) Apply to join a sea angling club if there is one anywhere near you; you will then have plenty of opportunities to make friends and obtain practical information; competitions and outings with fellow anglers also greatly add to your knowledge and experience.

(3) Learn all you can from the 'locals'; their ability to make good catches is often due to their knowledge of local conditions, such as wreck marks, tide eddies, any hot water outlets, and other specially favourable conditions.

(4) Serious thought could be given to taking out a personal and third-party risk insurance policy; for a very small premium one can obtain cover with many advantages. Insurance against loss or damage to rods can also be obtained at very little cost.

(5) Once you have obtained your primary essentials, it is a good idea to take them along to a quiet beach, or to a convenient field, and practise learning to cast, something you will need to master for beach and pier fishing, where some degree of accuracy is essential.

Five more worthwhile points that every good angler should bear in mind, and practise, are:

(1) Always inform someone when and where you are going fishing, and have some identity label attached to your tackle bag.

(2) Provide yourself with the necessary clothing so that at all times you can make yourself comfortable and avoid catching chills or colds.

(3) Learn about 'minimum sizes' and conform with the general body of good anglers who return to the sea all undersized fish of any species; this is important in order to conserve stocks.

(4) Always clean up your fishing position before you leave it,

by removing all rubbish, and leaving no trace of your visit.

(5) Having made an expensive outlay and possessing a fine set of new tackle, treat it with care and plan a methodical maintenance examination.

It is also important to become familiar with the subject of tides, as these will always influence fishing conditions and the decisions you make. If the following brief facts are understood, they may often be turned to advantage.

Tides are affected by the gravitational pull of both sun and moon. At full moon and new moon the pull is strongest, and thus we get the highest and lowest tides of the month, (springs); at the first and third quarters of the moon the pull is weakest, and we get the least difference between high and low tides, (neaps).

A tide flows for approximately six hours and then ebbs for about six hours, but does not ebb and flow over the ground at a uniform speed; in general, the water will rise (or fall) in this 123321 pattern:

1ft in the 1st hour	3ft in the 4th hour	—	When the
2ft in the 2nd hour	2ft in the 5th hour	—	rise or fall
3ft in the 3rd hour	1ft in the 6th hour	—	is 12ft

There is a short period of slack water at the turn of the tide, ie, between each change from the 'top of the tide' (full flood), to the 'run off', and from the end of the run off (full ebb) before the start of the 'flow in'. Note that a flowing tide, flood tide, and rising tide are synonymous terms for the general expression 'tide is coming in'; conversely, an ebb tide, or falling tide, is one that is 'going out'.

A flood tide is seen to be coming in as it creeps further up the beach, but it does not flow towards the shore so much as along it; when you cast in, the prevailing current will tend to take your tackle with it, in whichever direction it flows, (or ebbs). It will be the height of the tide that affects the strength of this current; thus a tide that rises 30ft will have three times the speed of one that only rises 10ft; though this is a factor which varies considerably from place to place.

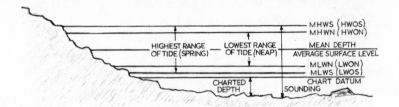

Fig. 1 Diagram showing tidal ranges

The above diagram will help you to understand the relevant terms describing tidal changes, and how tide is measured from a datum line.

The time of high tide increases by approximately half-an-hour every twelve hours; precise local times can be found in annual tide-tables, easily obtainable as a pocket folder card, quite cheap, and a necessity for any sea angler.

As the tide 'makes', or flows to cover more and more of the beach, that area becomes the sea bed and many small forms of marine life emerge from refuge. Many species of fish are aware of this transformation and follow the tide in to seek and devour anything tasty that may appear.

Should your interest lie in deeper waters, or extend over a large area, it is a good investment to procure a chart of the locality and note the varying state of the sea bed. It will show sandbanks, gullies, even wrecks, all of which, though hidden from view, will enable you to take advantage of the most suitable locations and be aware of the state of the bottom over which you are fishing. Sandy bottoms, for example, are the regular haunts of all kinds of flatfish, while sandy patches between weed-strewn, rocky beds hold an attraction for most species. Clean, rocky bottoms, on the other hand, usually contain little food, though any gullies between rocks could contain congers or lobsters.

Having examined some of the fundamental factors, we can

now turn to the practical side and consider the selection of a suitable rod and reel from the wide range of makes and materials available. All good anglers take pride in their rods and reels since, as well as constituting the. main control centre, they are the principal items of tackle, as well as the most costly.

SPLIT CANE rods, often called 'built cane', combine both strength and lightness, are quite flexible, yet at the same time maintain a firmness in their resiliency when in action.

WHOLE CANE rods are made in one piece, and being generally used for the cheaper type of rod, lack the precision that goes into the putting together of split cane rods. They are not really lively rods and though they can cope satisfactorily with the average size of fish, they are liable to become strained by a heavy weight or a mass of weed.

GREENHEART rods are definitely a good choice for beginners, and are made in many variations of thickness, length, and weight. They are heavier than split cane or fibreglass, and consequently much stiffer when in use. Their great advantage is that they will not rot nor take on set and become warped, and can withstand rough handling.

FIBREGLASS rods are of two distinct types, both of which enjoy great popularity: the 'hollow' type, which is very light and springy and makes an extremely good casting rod, and the 'solid' type, also quite springy but much more robust, and an excellent boat rod in the larger diameters. Both types are durable and very sensitive.

Hickory, bamboo, and other woods are also used in the making of many cheaper types of rod but, though often satisfactory, they are not in great favour and their low cost may sometimes turn out to be false economy.

With so many types of rods available in numerous sizes, one has first to consider which is likely to be best suited to the kind of fishing in prospect. To this end, they may be divided into the following categories according to their proposed use.

BEACH RODS. Here one needs to have casting power, a certain amount of flexibility, and sufficient strength to withstand heaving-in strongly. Under normal conditions a 9ft to 10ft rod, casting 3oz to 4oz, is a good beginning. You may cast further if you can manage one of 12ft to 14ft.

PIER RODS: Here the choice is much wider, as a walk along any pier at the right time will reveal. The most popular among the knowledgeable is a rod of from 7ft to 8ft, flexible enough to handle any strong snatch or sudden rush, yet possessing fairly good lifting power. It will need to be a little longer if distance casting is contemplated.

BOAT RODS: Casting being unnecessary and space often limited in small boats, the length varies, usually from 5ft to 7ft. It should be a well fitted, stout rod capable of driving home the distant strike and for lifting, if any large species are anticipated.

For spinning, drift-lining, or float fishing, a second lighter and much livelier rod is preferable, but purchase of these 'special-purpose' rods is best left until one becomes a devotee of one of these methods, other rods being meanwhile adapted for the purpose.

Obviously, then, one cannot define a 'general' type of rod to suit all purposes for the beginner and the best recommendation is for a single rod, 8ft to 9ft long, (7ft for boys), to cast up to about 6oz, selected for its quality rather than good looks. Once he has become dedicated to the sport, the keen angler will probably come to compromise with three types, which will suit practically all his requirements:

(1) A fairly stiff rod about 6ft to 7ft long, in two pieces; this is most suitable for use when fishing on the bottom, from boat or pier.

(2) A much lighter and more flexible rod, 7ft to 8ft long, pliable at the top to cope with fast runs and effective for casting; very suitable for pier fishing, and also useful for spinning and drift-lining.

(3) A sturdy rod in two pieces, as long as can be conveniently handled, to obtain maximum casting from a beach, and to heave in well.

Rod fittings are often overlooked or taken for granted, but they are really important, and should be carefully examined

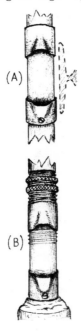

(A)

(B)

Fig. 2   Rod
fitting for reel

before accepting a rod. A good top is a 'must', and stainless steel is preferable. Rings of steel, agate, or porcelain, properly whipped and varnished, are all satisfactory, but do not accept porcelain if the fit is too loose, and remember that they should be removed at once if they become chipped in use.

The reel fitting should be of the adjustable screw locknut type as shown here (B), rather than the fixed plate and movable ring type (A) that can cause consternation when you least expect it. Make sure it is comfortably placed for use according to your stature, and that the handle is well encased by cork rings to form a convenient hand grip. A rubber cap fitted to the heel of the rod is also a necessity.

Also bear in mind when selecting your rod, that if you use nylon line, as most anglers do, and the rod is extra whippy, when you strike a bite you will have to cope with this bend in the rod in addition to overcoming the normal stretch of your line.

Next comes the most interesting item of the angler's equipment, the fishing reel, which is not so complicated or difficult to handle as it may at first appear. They come in three basic main types and in several sizes.

The CENTRE-PIN reel: This is a good general-purpose reel and ideal for casting if the drum is light. They are made in various materials and should be free-running, with minimal friction. The simplicity of their design ensures that a well-made one is practically trouble free, and they may be stripped open quite easily by pressing a small catch to release the locking key. The reel may then be lifted clear and the whole interior exposed for lubrication or cleaning out any sand that may have penetrated the mechanism. These reels are fitted with a check, which may easily be geared in or left clear by means of a flick switch.

The true centre-pin reel is one with the drum revolving on a shaft with a hardened key retainer, and without a nut to hold the drum on a spindle. The original 'Scarborough' reel, a wooden centre-pin, is considered the best type yet designed for general purposes, especially a large, robust one when there is a long drop to the water and the capture is likely to be heavy.

When boat fishing, some prefer using a 'Nottingham' type, which is somewhat similar but fitted with a drag as distinct from a check. If the drag is applied lightly, a snatched bait is more likely to be swallowed than if a check was on, transmitting vibrations which could cause the fish to drop the bait as it felt them. In either case, make sure that the reel you choose is the right size and weight to balance the rod.

Line tangles, resulting in 'bird's nests', are often a source of frustration to the beginner, but these can be avoided when casting by using a little thumb pressure on the reel edge to slow it down as the weighted tackle loses impetus and drops towards the water, eventually stopping it altogether as it hits the water.

Once the cast is released and away, keep an eye on the reel, and do not allow it to rotate faster than the line can reel off, otherwise the line will lift to form revolving bights which will eventually ride within each other, interlocking to form a tangle and jerk the reel to a stop (and perhaps snap the line in so doing). So keep your thumb on the rim edge as a brake and apply it firmly to slow it down, or even stop it altogether if you notice any sign of slack line on the reel.

The MULTIPLIER reel: This is an excellent reel for both long casting and spinning, and is generally accepted as being ideal for beach fishing, enabling a light weight to be used with a light line.

Only a small drum revolves, and the spool can be freed or geared in at the flick of a switch. In the better types, the handle remains stationary when casting, whilst the spool runs free, and when starting the retrieve, one turn will engage the spool which will automatically become geared in to revolve several times for each turn of the handle.

They are usually fitted with a slipping clutch and several other refinements, but being precision-made and durable, they tend to be expensive. There is a large selection to choose from, but bear in mind that some have limited winching powers, and a robust one is to be preferred.

The FIXED-SPOOL reel: This reel will throw a light weight a considerable distance without undue effort, and without risk of a 'bird's nest' as there are no revolving parts during a cast. To use it to best advantage, always keep the spool filled with line, and if it holds a lot it is usual to 'back it' by tying a length of discarded but usable line to the line proper and putting this on the reel first. Interchangeable spools are a handy feature of this type of reel, enabling one to replace broken lines in a jiffy or to fit one with a different breaking strain, and a slipping clutch is incorporated. Though ideal for beachcasting and spinning, when used for pier fishing where lifting a heavy catch may be necessary, a drop-net should always be used as these reels are definitely not designed for weight lifting.

To use the reel is quite a simple operation; first wind the weight up to its casting position and retain it there by finger control. Then, with everything clear for running, lift the bale arm up and back over to free the spool and cast in the normal way. When the bait hits the water, one turn of the handle will re-engage the spool and line may be reeled in to tauten to the weight.

When you make contact with a fish, two points to remember are that your reel is not designed to withstand excessive pressure, and that you should not continue reeling in when you feel the fish taking line from the spool, as this will only put turns in your line, which is something to avoid.

If your heavyweight turns out to be a mass of weed, it may necessitate 'pumping' the line in; ie, lowering and raising the rod to gather the slack line on to your reel. If, however, it is really heavily fouled, do not attempt to use the reel and strain its mechanism, but heave the line in hand over hand.

Despite this slight disadvantage, these reels are most popular for normal light-fish pier sport, and to assist your cast by a free running line, a larger first butt ring, about 18in from the reel, is an asset.

A fourth type of reel, not in general use but a personal preference among some anglers, is the SIDE-CASTING reel, so-called because the drum is positioned sideways, at right-angles to the rod while casting. The line spills out as in a fixed-spool reel, and after the cast is made the drum is repositioned to recover line and work as a centre-pin reel. Whichever type of reel is chosen, it should be overhauled frequently, using thin oil for lubrication as thick oil and grease tend to slow down their running.

Improved reel designs have produced new and greater capacity holders for all the types and lengths of line now available. The old-fashioned 'cuttyhunk' flax lines have been almost entirely superseded by synthetic materials for though they were good lines which became even stronger when wet, they had to be dried after use, which made them tiresome to look after. Twisted nylon is also obsolescent, having been much improved upon by monofilaments, though it is still used as a backing length for large reels.

Braided terylene lines are now among the most popular, their advantages being that they will not stretch under strain, will not damage the spool under pressure, cast exceedingly well

18

from multipliers, and are rot-proof. Most popular of all, however, is the single strand of nylon line, the monofilament threadline, whose smoothness permits a free continuous flow, especially when casting.

All types and qualities of line are easily obtainable on small drums in varying lengths and breaking strains, but the better quality lines are to be preferred as some of the cheaper brands are apt to be very springy and can weaken after being stretched in use. The lighter lines offer less resistance to the water, and your sport will be enhanced by using as light a line as possible. For the beginner, a length of 100yd of 12lb breaking-strain line would be quite suitable for a start.

After protracted use, all lines should be reversed, 'end for end', to prolong their useful life and carefully examined for any weaknesses which may have developed as the result of a snubbed cast, or a bird's nest.

A point to remember at this stage is that once the new line is off the maker's drum, you will have no indication other than touch of its breaking-strain; so make a note of it somewhere in case you need the information later on for making up traces, hook-ends, etc with part of it.

Having now studied rods, reels, and lines and made one's choice, only a weight is needed to complete the assembly of your main tackle and start to practise casting.

There is a wide variety of these in use, mostly of lead, as they are easy to make from patterned moulds. The beginner will soon appreciate that the weight of lead required is not governed by the size of the fish anticipated, but by the depth at which the fish are sought and the speed of the tidal current. And if fishing from a moving boat, its speed has also to be taken into account so that it may sometimes be necessary to change weights quite frequently. However, a range of 1oz to 4oz weights, plus a few heavier ones if strong tides are to be encountered, should be sufficient to start with, leaving other types to be added later according to experience and personal choice. A study of the drawing overleaf, showing the many types of weights available, will enable the beginner to appreciate their

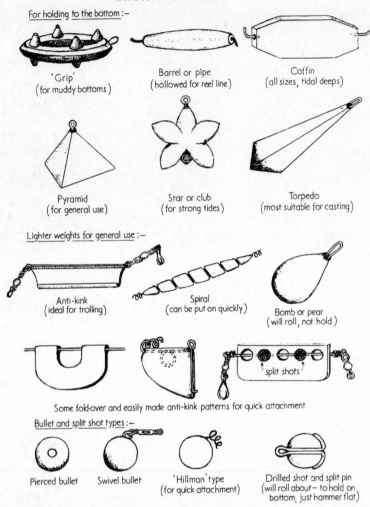

VARIOUS TYPES OF WEIGHTS

For holding to the bottom :—

'Grip' (for muddy bottoms)

Barrel or pipe (hollowed for reel line)

Coffin (all sizes, tidal deeps)

Pyramid (for general use)

Star or club (for strong tides)

Torpedo (most suitable for casting)

Lighter weights for general use :—

Anti-kink (ideal for trolling)

Spiral (can be put on quickly)

Bomb or pear (will roll, not hold)

split shots

Some fold-over and easily made anti-kink patterns for quick attachment

Bullet and split shot types :—

Pierced bullet

Swivel bullet

'Hillman' type (for quick attachment)

Drilled shot and split pin (will roll about – to hold on bottom, just hammer flat)

Fig. 3 Split shot may be pinched on but it is inadvisable to bite them on as teeth can transmit lead poisoning. Also remember, especially on rocky terrain, that old nuts and bolts, or pieces of old inner tubes filled with sand, are expendable substitutes

various uses and to select the one best suited for the prevailing conditions.

Incidentally, it is a good idea to keep your larger weights together on large split rings, to avoid dipping and diving into your creel or box for loose ones, whilst the smaller types for spinning and float fishing should have their own container.

There are many other types of weights not depicted, such as the Capta, similar to a drawn-out pyramid pattern and fitted with a top swivel; the watch type, similar to the Grip pattern but studless and without a centre hole; the large banana-shaped bulb-keeler pattern suitable for trolling; the flattened Kite lead that may be shaped for planing up off rocky bottoms; the pronged-torpedo casting type to obtain better anchoring hold, and several others.

The fitting of swivels is optional, and they can be useful for legering, but when using any type of anti-kink lead, always remember when fixing it to the reel line that the swivel goes below the lead to take the hook trace.

Weights, sinkers, leads and plummets, incidentally, are all synonymous terms.

CHAPTER 2

TERMINAL TACKLE AND ACCESSORY AIDS

Having considered rods, reels, and lines, the next important step is to study the various ways of making up the 'business end' of your tackle to attract and catch the fish.

There are many variations for different purposes—the less complicated the better as a rule—but there are half-a-dozen or so small fittings common to nearly all of them which you will need to use at some time or other in assembling your chosen presentation.

The cheapest yet most important item of your tackle, and the one on which much of your success will rely, is the hook. They come in many sizes, shapes and thicknesses, and are made with either straight or turned down eyes, or with flattened ends (called 'spade-end' hooks); they may be tinned or galvanised, but the best undoubtedly are those of stainless steel.

They may be bought loose, or already mounted on a nylon snood, and are graded according to size numbers, a system your dealer will gladly explain when you make your first purchase.

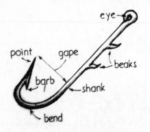

Fig. 4   Names applied to the various parts of a hook

Fig. 5   **Large** and small hooks fitted in tandem to retain long baits in position

Selection is determined by the type of fishing contemplated, eg, light sport such as spinning or driftlining needs a fine wire hook, whereas a heavy rod after a big fish calls for stout, heavy-gauge hooks. In all cases the size of the bait to be used must also be taken into account.

A good selection of various types of hooks will eventually be needed, so select them for quality rather than quantity, and always keep them in new condition, never mixing the old with the brand new. Examine those in use frequently, and discard them before they become old and rusty. And make sure they are kept sharp and not clogged by stale bait.

To complete the assembly of your choice, you will also require a selection of buckles, swivels, links, split rings, etc, for joining as necessary, to permit any quick change of tackle, and to obviate all possible twist in your gear. When not in use, all such spares should be kept in a special container, so that they are handy for replacements or to rig up any other pattern you may decide upon.

Here is a selection of such items, the use of each being obvious:

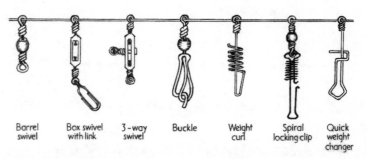

| Barrel swivel | Box swivel with link | 3-way swivel | Buckle | Weight curl | Spiral locking clip | Quick weight changer |

Fig. 6   Small items of tackle

The next subject to master is the knots one may safely use, and the methods of joining nylon together and securing your hooks. There are a dozen or so common knots and joins that meet most angling requirements. They are easy to make and safe in use and, once mastered, will give you an ample range of choice. Sailor's knots in general are not suitable for use with nylon owing to its smoothness, though they are very useful for cuttyhunk and flax.

The simplest form of hook tackle, or trace, is the single-hook-bottom. This is just a length of nylon with a hook at one end and an attachment loop at the other; it may be made with line of any breaking strain, to any length and to take any size of hook, and it is easily made up.

A half-dozen will be sufficient at first to stow in your bag, but later on you may find it convenient to add various others of different sizes and lengths for a special 'all-purposes' box. It is suggested that you do not begin to practise by cutting off the required lengths of nylon, but tie the hook on first while there is only one end to work with. Hold the hook in position with thumb and forefinger, then lay a loop along the shank and hold it there with your thumb; take the free end in your other hand and make half-a-dozen turns around both shank and loop, keeping them firmly in position without overlapping. Now push the end through the loop and gently tighten and form the knot by pulling both ends. When taut, slide it back to jam at the eye and then cut to the required length. Finally, form an attachment loop on the other end and trim off.

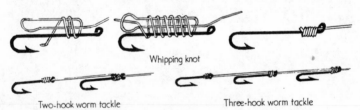

Fig. 7   Making-up single-, two- and three-hook worm traces

The 'yard-bottom' is a commercial size, ie, 3ft long, whilst others of 18in or 12in are available, but you can now make as many as you wish, with any size hook, breaking strain or length of nylon, at the cost of only a few pence each.

An effective and attractive arrangement when baiting up with a large worm is the 'two-hook worm-tackle', the spaced hooks serving to keep the worm extended and active, and at the same time presenting less bait for a fish to take without encountering a hook.

To make this, begin by proceeding as for the yard-bottom, but in making the initial loop, double back an extra long end so that when the knot is completed there is a workable length remaining where normally you would trim off. The second hook is now tied on by this end, using the same method, and placing it about 2in from the first one. To make a three-hook worm-tackle, double back a still longer length at the start on the first hook.

There are several other knots for securing a hook to nylon, each angler having his own preferences, and some of the more

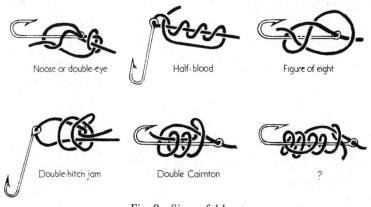

Noose or double-eye   Half-blood   Figure of eight

Double-hitch jam   Double Cairnton   ?

Fig. 8   Six useful knots

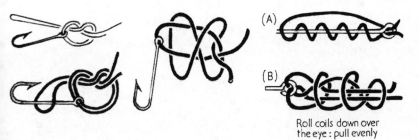

(A)

(B)

Roll coils down over the eye : pull evenly

The double grip knot

Figs. 9, 10, 11   Other methods of securing a hook to nylon

popular ones are shown here, formed before tightening the knot.

If you practise some of these with a bit of string first, and then nylon, you may eventually find the one you prefer most, but they will all do the job required.

Another knot you should know of, unconnected with securing hooks, is the 'overhand' knot, (A below) which should not be used for joining with nylon as it will come apart under the slightest strain. It can, however, be reliable if made into a 'double overhand', as at (B), and has some minor uses, as at (C) for instance, when securing your line to your reel, to retain the end.

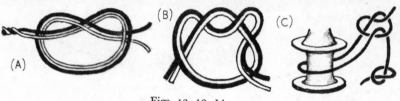

Figs. 12, 13, 14

Next to consider is the loop at the end of your yard-bottom, or home-made trace, for its attachment as part of your end tackle. Or, if preferred, you can make a loop in the end of the reel line itself. These are easily formed, as shown below, but always remember never to use a bowline with nylon, as it will tend to slip. Both the following are in general use, the Flemish loop being preferred.

Flemish loop   Ring knot

Fig. 15   Methods of attaching reel line or trace to end tackle

When it comes to joining two nylon ends (line and trace) together, there is no doubt that the best knot for this purpose is the 'blood-knot'. This is formed as shown below; then, holding the two ends, snug the coils up together neatly, pull them close, and when formed tighten all four parts and trim off.

Two other methods where loops are used frequently, are the 'strap bend', used to interlock two bights and called 'cowheeling', and the 'ring hitch', often called the 'lark's head', which is used to secure an attachment loop to swivels, buckles, or other eyes.

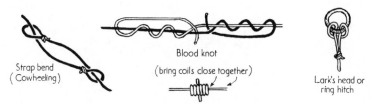

Strap bend
(Cowheeling)

Blood knot

(bring coils close together)

Lark's head or
ring hitch

Fig. 16   How to join two nylon ends together

Now to set about assembling some of the different types of tackle used, and since most species of fish feed on or near the sea bed, the primary decision is whether the bait should be on or just off the bottom. This will depend upon what species may be about, or the particular quarry you may have in mind, and as the techniques differ, let us examine both and the gear used for each.

The Paternoster: Briefly, this is a rig whose extreme end is a weight which will rest on the bottom and suspend the bait(s) in the area just above it. Thus, in any of its varying forms, the paternoster is the tackle for deliberately fishing 'just off the bottom'.

A study of their assembly in the illustrations will show how they offer a very simple method of fishing using quite simple gear; note that the hook links are shown at varying angles for clarity, though of course they do not stand out like that when submerged, but vary with tides and distance cast.

The simplest form of pater (A), consists of a lead at the bottom of the line, and two or more hooks attached by short lengths of nylon (called snoods) where required. One disadvantage here is that the hooks may become entwined with the main line, and snag up, when used for casting.

The boom-type pater (B), helps to overcome this failing by the use of rigid arms to extend and keep the hooks clear of the

27

line; these arms, or booms, may be of perspex, brass, or stainless steel, about 8in long, and are so affixed that they jut out at right angles to carry a short snood, 4in to 6in, in length, to try to avoid the tiresome repetition of untangling caught-up hooks.

Swivels should be fitted to the trace both above and below each boom.

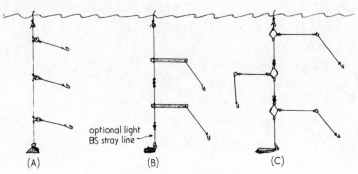

optional light
BS stray line

(A)   (B)   (C)

Fig. 17   Three types of paternoster

The straight-pull boom-pater (C), is a great improvement and one of the most popular available, but do not have the snoods too long.

If fishing over sand or mud the lower hook may be near the lead, or it could be raised if desired, whilst over rocky ground it should be raised to keep the whole assembly high enough to avoid snagging up.

In all types of paternosters it is advisable to use a small length of light nylon to secure the weight and act as a weak link if the lead should get caught up on the bottom. If, then, when you heave and something has to give, you will lose only the weight and the pater itself should survive. This then is the basic paternoster principle, a tackle that can be lowered and kept at any required depth, suspended by a float, or used in any techniques where one wishes to keep off the bottom.

Some anglers prefer to dispense with the use of booms and spreaders and, if using any variation of the original (A), may find it convenient to affix snoods to selected positions above the weight by making a 'dropper' where needed. This is simply a firmly positioned loop put in the pater to take either the hook direct, a snood, or a permanent swivel for a snood, as shown below:

Optional

Pull coils together

Fig. 18   Making a dropper

For normal fishing two hooks are enough, but for deep water, a longer pater with three, well spaced, will be better and permit the use of a variety of baits.

The Paternoster Trot: This is simply a single hook mounted well above the weight, with the lower hook(s) strung out on a trace as a trot. All the measurements may be varied, both for spacing and depth. It is inclined to be cumbersome and susceptible to tangling if one becomes too ambitious and adds three or four hooks, especially when casting, but it will stream out well when lowered into a tideway. When used with just a single

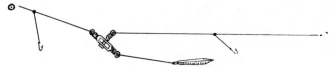

Fig. 19   A paternoster trot

hook on the trace, and one well up, as illustrated, it is quite a successful method and is recommended to the beginner for his first trials.

The Running Paternoster: This rig is invariably used for long-range casting and enables one to keep the bait off the bottom at a predetermined depth, (A) while the line is free to run through the swivel eye attached to the thin depth line holding the weight. In the diagram a second hook has been added to the trace, but this is optional.

A popular variant of the running paternoster can be rigged up, as shown at (B). A single hook trace is used, the second hook being positioned further up the line as required, and the long trace running through the weight swivel. The distance it can run is checked by the positioning of the two beads, but make sure that the upper bead is below the arc of the swinging hook.

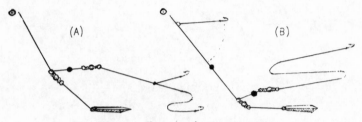

Fig. 20   Two running paternosters

The Sliding Paternoster: This consists of a small plastic or metal boom, or any other fitting, such as those shown here, which may be carried loose, unfitted, in your bag until wanted. The idea is that they may be easily attached to the line, and moved up or down to plumb all depths.

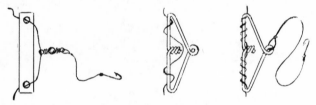

Fig. 21   Two sliding paternosters

A small trace or snood is attached once it is in position, to swirl around clear of any crabs or rocks; one is of the 'thread it on first' type, and the other a ready-use one to attach to the line as needed.

The Wandering Paternoster: This is an interesting and unorthodox method which can be used for a little diversion when things seem quiet. All that is needed is a small hook-length of 3ft or so, a buckle for attachment to the line, and a small shot or rubber band stopper placed above the end-tackle down on the bottom already; (this is put on about 3ft above

before sending your normal tackle down). The wandering trace
is clipped on to the main line by a buckle, (A) and then streamed
out, a gentle shaking of the rod facilitating its gradual descent
down the line. It will cover much ground before reaching the
stopper, and a bite here will produce a peculiar effect as you
feel a fish swimming along your line (B).

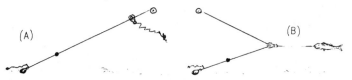

(A)   (B)

Fig. 22   The wandering paternoster

Paternosters may be used from either pier, shore, or boat.
The use of a larger hook on the. bottom is considered good
practice, whilst swivels may be fitted to suit one's own designs,
usually where a fish can get a direct pull. But don't overdo it,
as they can collect weed.

The use of two hooks on one trace is often decried on the
grounds that 'you can't catch two fish at once', or 'they are
bound to foul each other', but there are three good reasons
why it is worthwhile to use them when conveniently possible.
If the fish has torn a bait from the hook, yet not felt the metal
hook, it may well attack the other. Or if you lose a bait when
casting, or perhaps have had one taken, there is still one baited
hook left and you are not wasting your time.

Paters may be cast well out or lowered underfoot at a chosen
spot, and if fitted with a bomb weight can be permitted to roam
as well. They can also be used quite successfully with floats.

Legers: Legering differs from paternoster methods in that
the main object is to keep the weight always on the bottom,
instead of at varying depths as in other techniques, so that the
bait is retained on or close to the sea bed where most fish feed.

The Fixed Boom and Trace: This is an easy, straightforward method of anchoring a bait and confining it to one spot;
the type of boom (any kind or pattern may be used), the weight
itself, traces and swivels, may all be varied according to con-

ditions. The advantages of using a boom are threefold in that as well as keeping the trace clear when casting, it permits a fish to pull the line almost direct (and indicate this to you by rod tip movement), and also provides a small area for the initial sampling and biting before actually feeling the weight.

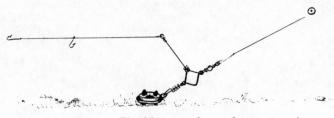

Fig. 23   Fixed boom and trace leger

The Running Line and Leger: This is a somewhat similar method to the previous one, but in this case the metal leger (of which there are many patterns), has the reel line running

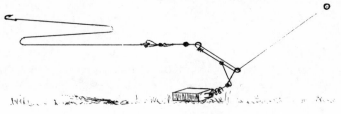

Fig. 24   A running leger

through it. This allows the line and trace to run off freely to cover more ground, as far as you wish, and a biting fish will not feel the weight, as there is no direct connection.

The Roving Bait Leger: This method differs from the running line and leger only in the type of weight used, a pear-shaped (Arlesey) bomb lead being fitted to enable the weight, and the run-through trace, to be carried around by tidal conditions over a very large area, (as in (A). This is a useful method when fishing a sandy or shingle bottom free of obstructions; if over large shingle, and the bomb fails to roll, change to a pipe or barrel lead.

32

Fig. 25   The roving bait leger

It can be seen that by placing a short length of nylon on the weight, it will change into a running pater off bottom, the 'stray line' added being your depth setting for a 'streaming trace', (as in (B)).

The Paternoster Leger: This is a good rig for beach casting, as the weight retains the trace on the bottom, with a pater running out from it, and the fish does not have to shift the lead before you get the message.

Fig. 26   The paternoster leger

Three hooks may be used if you can manage a moderately long trace, the largest one being on the end; use a casting type lead.

The Double Running Leger: This is one of those variants sometimes used, in which it will be seen that both hooks are acting separately as independent running legers.

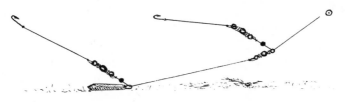

Fig. 27   The double running leger

33

It could be useful when it can be streamed clear from a pier or a boat, but when casting there will be some risk of entanglement.

Having now assembled your tackle and being ready to start fishing, you obviously require something to keep all the items together for transportation.

The Creel, or Fishing Bag: Many angler's bags are a mystery even unto themselves, everything being crammed in willy-nilly where it stays put until next time out, when the inevitable unscrambling process begins before tackling up. Some like it that way, but the methodical angler will prefer the systematic planning of his portable hold-all, the general aim being a carrier that is strong, roomy, as light as possible, and capable of transporting all that one may need for either a long or short session on beach or pier, or a dinghy trip.

The first step in such a plan would be to list all the equipment you are likely to want in your locality, and then recheck it. Next one could procure a varied assortment of small containers, eg, plastic boxes, tins, tubes, and round screw-top tins (preferably with a turning lever to open). Each receptacle will contain similar items—all spoons in one, spare hooks in another, and so on—and if each is a different shape and colour, once you have memorised them, any one will be easy to find, especially in the dark.

In addition to the normal items such as reels, weights, spare spools, etc, and your collection of small containers, there are some other items worth considering as optionals for inclusion.

First, and almost essential, is a small first-aid container, which could contain a square of lint, bandages and safety pins, a small bottle of antiseptic, scissors, and some Elastoplast, the whole wrapped in a cotton-wool bundle to shape into its container and sealed in a plastic bag.

Other items include a cloth roll to hold bait knife, disgorger, booms, pliers, etc together; spring balance, corks, ferrule lubricant, floats, sliding paters, and spare spools, all in containers if possible. Now place the lot together, stacked up as if in a bag, add essentials such as reels, a shallow bait box, hand

34

towels, bag for your catch, flask for tea or soup, and sand-wiches container (these last two might go in your coat pocket, or in an exterior pocket at each end of your bag), and you will then have some idea of the size of the bag you will need.

There are several types in the shops, such as the old-fashioned wicker creel, haversacks, bass bags, and wood or metal boxes containing sliding trays and compartments, or, you could con-sider adapting one of the many types of shopping bags, with or without zipped sidepockets, or even make up a canvas bag or wooden box to your own ideas.

Having decided which type suits you best, make sure that it will take all your gear with some space to spare and that it has either a shoulder strap or can be carried without the handles cutting into your hands when full. It should be waterproof if possible, or at least have a waterproof top flap and if possible, line the inside base with a wooden rectangle, say $\frac{3}{4}$in thick, as stiffener, and attach to it two exterior cross-battens, 1in thick, to keep the whole clear of any wet decks.

The Rod-Rest: This is a 'must' for the beach angler, and on most other occasions other than in a boat where one has to hold the rod continuously.

Some decry its use on the grounds that many fish are lost because they drop the bait before one can lift and strike, whilst many are apt to misuse it in that they just cast out, tighten the line, put the rod in the rest, and leave the fish to ring the bell to let them know that they have been and gone. Nevertheless for taking a rest when your arms ache, a food break, sheltering from the rain, and rebaiting, a rest can be a boon, and far better than laying the rod down on the beach with the risk of sand entering the reel mechanism. There are a number of types available, or they are easy to knock up at home. They should not be so flimsy that a good wind can capsize the whole lot, and the most useful are 4ft to 5ft high, to keep the rod up steeply and your line clear of any breakers. The tripod designs are best for use on shingle beaches, and the spiked single rod upright type for sandy positions.

The Gaff: This is another necessity for the bigger fish, and can be useful on the beach or rocks, as well as in a boat. It comprises a sharp hook affixed to a stout handle to enable the angler to transfer the weight of the fish from his line so that he may manhandle the fish to bring it in. The tapered, needle-sharp hook should be of a stout metal, not likely to open under strain, and be securely fastened to a fairly long handle; a safety loop is usually fitted (thick enough not to cut the hand).

The gaff is put in near the gills, firmly and deliberately, to bring the hook through the fish when the weight is transferred from the rod. Keep rod, line and trace well clear to prevent the fish tangling the lot up for you as you lift it in, as rods have been broken, and even lost in these circumstances.

If you are thinking of getting a gaff of the screw-on type, remember that they are liable to unscrew as easily as they screw on, when all could be lost; and whichever type you obtain, keep the point embedded in cork when not in use.

The Landing Net: This useful accessory is a weighted net about 18in deep, secured to a metal frame which may be circular, triangular, or half-moon shaped, and fitted to a light strong handle. In use, it is placed in the water, submerged until it assumes its shape, and then the fish is gradually drawn towards it until, when over it, the rim is lifted up clear of the water. If the fish is a large one for the size of the net, the answer is to get the head in first and lift the net in the direction of its body.

For use on piers, the same net may easily be converted into a drop-net by removing the handle and securing a bridle and buoyrope to the rim. Here, the net is usually kept in the water all the time one is fishing, ready for immediate use. The procedure is similar, except that it is more difficult to work the net into position by rope than with a handle, especially when it may be some distance down to the water. A large rim helps to make things easier, whilst submerging and lifting is preferable to trying to scoop the net about. Remember to examine the condition of your net from time to time, especially the bottom, as many a good fish has been lost by breaking through a rotten net while being lifted from the water.

CHAPTER 3

PUTTING THEORY INTO PRACTICE

Let us now make two hypothetical expeditions, one to a beach and another to a pier or jetty, as a step-by-step introduction for the beginner who may still be in doubt about the procedure to adopt.

Fishing from a beach. Assume that you have arrived on a typical sandy or shingle beach; the tide which was 'out' has just turned and is now beginning to cover the still wet low-tide area. For the next five hours or so, as the tide rises and approaches you, you will be retreating slowly up the beach, so start by selecting a favourable position, fairly well back.

Position your rod rest; now set up your chosen rod for casting, fit your reel, run your line through the rod rings, and finish by adding a buckle to the attachment loop in the end of your line. Then place the rod in its rest while you study the local conditions to determine which is the best gear and method to use (see page 50).

A decision made, you now select the trace, lead weight, etc, arranged as pater or leger, and secure this 'end tackle' to the reel line. See that the whole runs freely and hangs clear in a free-running position from the rod tip, leaning on the rest, ready for the bait.

Bait-up your hooks now if you have carried out your casting tests previously; otherwise, leave the baiting-up process awhile until you have made a few practice casts with weight only, so as to get the feel of things.

For this casting practice take up a convenient position at the water's edge, and at your first effort do not try to span fifty or a hundred yards. Just relax, take it easy, and start your trials

37

with short easy casts, avoiding all jerky movements; correct control is the secret of casting, rather than brute force.

There are two popular styles in general use, the 'side swing' and the conventional 'overhead' cast. Although the former is useful and favoured by some, you will be well advised to keep to the overhead method at first, as directional control is easier and it will give you better distances as you improve later on.

Take a comfortable relaxed stance, facing half-right (vice versa if left-handed), and reel in slowly until the weight hangs freely suspended about 2ft from the rod tip. Retain it in this position by finger control, pressing the line to the rod, or with the thumb holding the reel stationary to prevent it running off until released.

Turning slightly to the right, hold the rod to extend behind the body, opposite to the direction of your proposed cast and parallel to the ground with the weight suspended just clear of it. Assuming you are using a fixed-spool reel, free the spool by lifting the bale arm over and make sure that all is set to run off freely.

To cast, the rod tip is brought up over the right shoulder in an arc until it points straight in front of you, and remember that the spring in the rod is there to impel your end tackle, rather than any great force. When you are ready and have made sure that no one is standing too close to you, raise both arms and the horizontal rod about a foot, together, and with a steady, firm, quick thrust with the upper hand bring the rod smartly over your head in the direction required. When the swing is at its maximum and the rod about to point seawards, release the line and your tackle is speedily on its way.

As the lead begins to lose its velocity and height, with any reel other than a fixed-spool, you must gradually brake the reel with your thumb to decrease the speed of the line running off it, or it may coil back on itself to 'bird's nest'. Check the line fully for a moment as the weight takes the water, and while it sinks move to your fishing position, recovering any spare line by reeling in until you feel the pull of the weight. Continue with the practice until you feel reasonably confident.

When you are ready to start fishing, bait-up your hooks, cast out, tauten your line, and adjust your drag or reel check to ensure that a bite will not pull your rod into the sea if for any reason you should leave it unattended in the rod rest. Set your rod up in its rest and try this out.

You will soon discover the best position for balancing and holding your rod comfortably whilst maintaining light finger control on the line, and if your tackle should be gradually moving away, a heavier weight may be needed to combat the current and retain it in position. You can now picture how the baits on your pater are streaming out, or your leger swirling the baits around, according to its length.

If things get a bit slow, it may sometimes help to reel in a couple of turns at short intervals; as the lead drags through the sand it makes a cloudy disturbance to which any feeding fish in the vicinity might be attracted, and this process can be repeated until it becomes necessary to recast.

Slight twitchings on the line may be caused by marauding crabs, or weed, so if using a soft bait, reel in and examine it frequently. But if at any time you feel a definite pluck or tug, raise the rod tip, tauten your line by taking one or two turns on the reel, and pause slightly. If there is no resistance or movement, continue reeling in, as a fish may be swimming towards you, but at the same time be prepared to permit line to run off should it be a big one. The occasional tight line pause when reeling in should enable you to feel if you have a fish on.

If there was some resistance, and the pressure persists without signs of movement, you may possibly have hooked a mass of seaweed; in any case you should reel in and examine your bait. If the pressure is inert and also fairly heavy, lay the rod in its rest and recover your tackle by hauling in 'hand over hand'; do not strain your rod and its fittings.

If however your strike was a successful one, your rod tip will show activity and you will feel the distant movements of the fish as you automatically tauten the line and reel in. Do it smoothly, as keeping the line taut is more important than speed, and if he is a bit heavy play it cool when he tugs or pulls;

hold him, yield if you have to, recover line when you can, but try not to let the line go slack or he may become unhooked and get away. If he is a really heavy one, or a fighter, you may have to resort to the method of 'pumping him in', ie, lower the rod to sea level, hold the reel drum, raise the rod vertical to bring him nearer, then lower the rod and reel in simultaneously to recover line, and go on repeating these movements.

As you bring your fish nearer the beach, watch out for any undertow, and if there is any, hold the line against it and then reel in with the incoming surf. When the fish is sighted, use any surf that there is, walk backwards a little, then lift it clear of the water and turn to swing it on to the beach, well up clear of the water's edge.

The first thing to do now is to identify what you have caught, and you should not touch it except with your boot (not with a shoe), until you are sure. Common catches such as pouting, flatties, etc, may be unhooked forthwith, but any that can bite or sting, such as congers or weevers, should be killed on the hook, so unbuckle the used tackle and detach it with the fish on, if you are at all doubtful.

Once you have recast with new tackle and bait, stand the rod in its rest, attend to the reel, and fit a small bell to the rod tip. This bite detector is a useful accessory when you have to leave the rod for any purpose; just clip it on to the rod near the tip, and any bite should ring it.

During the course of your session here, continually retreating before the advancing tide, recourse can be made to interchanging various forms of tackle and baits to ascertain which you find easiest to handle, and which baits prove most successful under varying conditions.

When you decide to pack up, reel in and clean off your hooks, wipe off traces of weed anywhere, restow your bag and take a careful look around before you leave to make sure that no hooks or nylon lengths have been left lying about.

Fishing from a pier or jetty. For our second hypothetical session, let us assume you are on the pier of your choice. Noting the position of shelters, railings, etc, select a suitable point from which to try some bottom fishing, using a pier rail for a rod rest if possible.

Set up your tackle, attach a weight and send it down to test it in the running current; if it will not hold its position replace it with a heavier one.

Now attach and bait-up your leger or pater, with a different bait on each hook, and see that all is clear for running before you cast out. If the pier is crowded, or you are not too confident of your casting ability, you will be well advised to adopt the 'underhand pendulum' swing-out, or simply lower the tackle straight down into the water. When the lead is on the bottom, tighten your line to it and put on the reel check (NOT the drag); do this also if you have been able to make a long cast. If using a fixed-spool reel, see that the slipping clutch button (on top) is so adjusted that line may be pulled off easily; ie, not turned right back so that it can run free, or set so tight that the line will tend to pull the rod instead of unwinding on the reel.

You can now settle down into a comfortable position, holding your rod as most convenient, with the line under finger-tip control for a bite to be felt as it pulls on the rod tip. Meanwhile, remember always to keep your bait wrapped up and do not spread your other gear all over seats others may wish to use.

If at times you want to lean your rod against the rail to free your hands for some purpose, always bear in mind the following points: lay two-thirds of your rod inboard, with only the tip over the rail; see there is no drag on at all, as you do not want that big fish to topple your rod and ditch it; put on your check if you have one, so that you will hear the reel turn as the fish snatches, or if you have no check then fix a bell to the tip as a warning indicator. Also make sure your line can be pulled off once the rod tip has bent, by an almost free setting of your slipping clutch, and test this out before you leave the rod. If your spool has little line on, or you are proposing to leave it set up for some while, consider tying a slip knotted cord or hand-kerchief round both rod and rail.

The actual fishing, striking, reeling in and so on are much

the same as when beach fishing, except that various other methods can be tried out and you can see more of what is happening below you. The one great difference appears when you hook a large fish, as now you are unable to swing it round and drop it on a beach, but have to get it from the water up to where you are standing, and possibly over a rail.

If using a fixed-spool reel this may be nigh impossible without the aid of a dropnet, but if you do not have one with you, then lower your rod tip towards the water, grasp the reel and line firmly, and if your tackle is of good quality you should make a successful lift. Alternatively, lay down your rod and haul it up 'hand over hand'; do not jerk, and prevent it touching anything on the way up to lever itself off, as fish can often do.

Changing of weights with the varying current, frequent examination of the baits, a decision to change tackle, and many other things will keep your time occupied until a fish obliges. Should you get caught up in any obstruction under water, and swearing and a firm steady pull will not free you, lay down your rod and grasp the line beyond its tip; gradually stretch the line, try an occasional quick springy release, and then try this from either side at an angle. If something gives it should be the lighter breaking-strain stray line securing the weight, leaving the rest of your gear intact.

Let us now examine those controversial problems of how and when to strike, and how to play the fish from the bite to its exhaustion and ultimate capture.

Skilled anglers realise that small hooks require less striking effort than the larger ones, because the points are finer and sharper and the barb relatively smaller, but with all sizes a strike is more effective when part of the hook and the barb are fully exposed so make sure there is not too much bait clogged around the barb to hamper effective penetration.

The beginner has to learn to be patient and not swipe the rod tip up six feet every time something touches his line. Wave movements will bounce his lead about as it surges here and there; there may be the gentle twitching drag of a crab or a fouling of the line by a clump of weed; in all these instances there is an absence of a real tug or snatch, and therefore no need to strike.

A knowledge of how the different species react when attracted to a bait will help to distinguish between a genuine bite and a false alarm. First let us consider the flatfish species. With these, striking is not only unnecessary but usually bad practice, for these fish will invariably hook themselves by swallowing the bait, a process that often takes some time because of their small mouths. The first sign of a nibble may move the rod tip, yet the fish may have only a light hold of the bait, whilst the hook is not even in its mouth. To pull it out means a lost fish.

Codling give a sharp bite, as do whiting and pouting, whilst the 'knock' of a bream is a distinct tug; eels give a jerky tug, and all of these should be struck as soon as they are felt. Although these types may sometimes hook themselves, the angler holding his rod and keeping a taut line will undoubtedly be more successful than his neighbour who may be content to rely on a bell, or some other device, as a reminder whilst he takes his rest.

Bass will sometimes hook themselves, but generally their bite will be a tap, tap, followed by a swift rush away; strike these hard on the run. Conger invariably nudge the bait about a bit, gently nibbling or mouthing it, which may cause a few line vibrations, but when he starts really moving away with it, then make a determined strike. Tope are diffident in their biting habits, but their rush off with the bait has nothing uncertain about it; they often turn and swim towards you, so recover line quickly and strike hard at the first chance.

The first indication of a fish taking the bait will be felt through your finger-tip control on the line, when simultaneously the line will tend to straighten, pulling your rod into a bend in the process. Instinctively you strike by raising your rod tip to drive home the barb of the hook; then lower the tip quickly, reeling in the gathered line until it is horizontally straight out. Pause slightly to feel if you have anything on; raise your rod to tauten the line, and if uncertain reel in quite a few turns, watching to see if the rod tip is being twitched or pulled. These actions are all performed in quick succession, and even if you feel no resistance, do not despair as the fish may be running towards you. So go on reeling in quickly, hoping that he is still 'on'. If it does prove to be a miss, your bait will need attention anyway, and after a time you will quickly learn to sense a 'yes' or 'no'.

Mullet, if any are about, need only a gentle, quick strike so do not be too rough or you may tear the hook away from the soft fleshy mouth, and special care is needed in bringing them in towards you.

As one is obviously unaware which species is after your bait, though one can often hazard a guess, try to remember how the bite felt as your skill will be greatly enhanced if you know what you have on your hook before sighting it.

Having gained an insight into when and how to strike, let us now consider how to make the fullest use of the facilities afforded by your tackle for playing the fish in and ensuring its capture.

Modern rods, reels, and lines, are all so designed to help cushion the sudden strain of a hard strike, or the jerk of a large fish swooping at speed, which might otherwise break the line. Properly used, this combination makes for selective control and adds power to your efforts. The rod may be elevated or lowered to give or take distance, the line eased, held, or reeled in, or the drag adjusted to brake a little and make the fish pull harder. Thus, and allowing for the normal stretching of the line under these circumstances, the angler is able to keep his quarry under constant strain with every move it makes without risk of that sudden jerk or overstrain that could snap his line.

Conversely, to examine the process from the fish end as it strikes at the bait, it has (1) to straighten the sag in the trolled line; (2) the line is now longer than it was, as the jerk of the bite has taken up the elasticity of the line; (3) the rod now works to the strain of the fish and shows resistance in its bending, and (4) if the drag has been set 'on', the strike will have straightened the line, stretched it, and bent the rod before an inch of line has left the reel. So the fish must now pull against the drag of the reel and start it turning, and the angler must manipulate his tackle accordingly.

Most normal sized fish can be reeled in gradually without too much effort, but if one starts your reel turning or there are other indications that you have a whopper, then the procedure will be different and both strength and patience may be needed to control him. The great thing at this moment is to restrain any instinctive impulse to hold him at any cost, or to put your drag on to the limit. To do so will only defeat your object, as it will make all your tackle effort rigid instead of springy, and you could quickly part your line.

If the fish wants to reel off line, let it do this against your pre-set drag; keep your rod pointing upwards so that it will expend more energy bending it. Then, when opportunity offers, slow it down by adding gradually to the brake pressure, yielding only to a really heavy pull or sudden jerk, until you are able to stop and turn it. Should the line suddenly go slack, it does not necessarily mean that you have lost your fish, it may be swimming your way (bass and tope frequently adopt this tactic), so reel in and quickly retrieve all the line you can.

Once you have stopped him, and this may take some time, you must start bringing him in towards you. Point your rod towards him at water level, grasp both reel and line, and begin 'pumping him in' by raising the rod almost vertically, then reeling in quickly to gather the slackened line as you lower the rod again; keep repeating this action.

This 'give and take' could continue for some time, and remember never to reel in whilst he is taking line or to overstrain your rod or reel. So never be afraid to yield a little now and again, and eventually the fish will begin to tire and you will find him coming closer with every pump you make.

As he nears you, keep your rod well up and out, clear of anything that would afford him leverage and the chance to break away. Make sure you have a net or gaff handy, and that any spare rods or tackle are well out of the way.

In a small boat it may be advisable to bring your catch in over the stern rather than amidships, where the resultant commotion has been known to cause a capsize; if it is a conger, stun it, kill it, and put it in a sack.

Successful angling, then, means obtaining the maximum advantage from the gear at your disposal, and most of the difficulties beginners experience result from using a fixed-spool reel which is not strong enough for its job, or when the angler is unfamiliar with the setting of his slipping clutch or drag and allows so much strain to build up that something has to go, including the fish. So make sure that you not only know how your gear works, but try it out on land by attaching the hook to a fixed position and familiarising yourself with the pull of the line from the reel with the drag set at different tensions.

CHAPTER 4

WHERE, WHEN AND HOW TO FISH

There are many different methods of sea fishing: surface fishing, bottom fishing, beach, pier, or jetty fishing, boat fishing, spinning, drift-lining, trolling, whiffing, float fishing, and many others, each of which may call for different kinds of end tackle, different ways of using them, and quite often a different kind of bait.

This chapter is devoted to short descriptions of some of these methods and of the techniques to be employed. Later, more specialised forms of angling will be considered, such as catching the wily mullet, bass hunting, and similar pursuits of specific quarries which are often taken up to the exclusion of all others.

PIER OR JETTY FISHING

Some anglers are very successful in this whilst others rarely seem to catch any worthwhile fish. Note that many piers are frequently adorned by their 'regulars' who, being well aware of where and when fish congregate, know which positions to choose and which to avoid. So never be averse to studying them, or better still, seeking information.

The best time to start is in April, if mild, otherwise in May. It is wise to first ascertain if there is a ban on overhead casting, night fishing, use of feathers, or if certain areas are out of bounds, as is the case on some piers; it will also pay dividends if you first explore the area round the pier at low tide, making a mental note of all inlets, gullies, rocky patches and other obstructions on the sea bed.

At low water half the pier is usually devoid of water, so for the first hour of a rising tide, with only the pierhead to fish from, casting as far as possible out into deep water may be the only way to make contact with a fish coming in with the tide. At the same time it could be profitable to try out your dropnet, for prawns which can later be used as bait.

As the water deepens, start to move inshore with the tide, along the side of the pier, casting out a little, reeling in a few turns now and again to cover more ground, and then leger along the piles; alternating a two-hook pater with a 3ft single hook trace and spiral. Later on, you can try casting further afield as the tide reaches halfway. A change of bait to hermit crab or squid on at least one hook could vary your offerings as you gradually keep moving inshore, for remember, the fish also are moving in with the tide.

About an hour before high water, in a position just behind the surf, you may now bait up with that tasty morsel you have kept for that big one you know is there. Stay in this spot until the flood is full, but as the tide turns and starts to run off, retreat along the pier with it, casting in different areas as you go, for it is usually possible to take fish during the next three hours during the run-off, though when the water shallows they usually leave the area in a hurry.

It is seldom necessary to cast your tackle too far from the pier sides; down tide you can arrange for it to be carried a long way, but up tide it will tend to return in your direction, so about 25yd is ample, and then gradually reel in until fishing almost under the rod tip. Often a bite will be felt when reeling in; if so do not stop, try a firm strike and reel on until you are sure the fish has the hook. Reel in steadily as fish will often follow a bait and make the final bite as they see it tend to rise and leave the water.

Fishing on the sunny side of a pier is best for mullet and species that love warm water, but in the shade the fish will often congregate round the girders and piles, where the weed festoons hold the food that attracts small fry, which, in turn attract the larger species.

If the area is surrounded by rocky pools, home of sandeels

and prawns, try a float tackle, but if the bottom is sand or mud, leger with worms. And when using worms, do not screw them up into a ball on the hook, but mount them hooked lightly through the head, to stream out naturally as if being carried by the current.

If you settle for an hour or so in an apparently favourable position, ground bait may help; place it in a small sack skewered with a few holes and hang it in the water a few feet off bottom. If mackerel are about, then adjust your tackle to swim just below the surface, using a lask as bait, whilst if pollack are around they often succumb to float tackle, particularly at dusk when they tend to rise.

When starting the pier season, keep on or near the bottom and be content with one hook per rod for a better catch and fewer tangled traces. On warm summer evenings, when cool breezes just ruffle the surface, it will often be worth while working a large area with a float, but if there are rollers running in, change to leger in the backscour.

Whenever things tend to get quiet, maintain your interest by methodically spending a few minutes over the wide gaps between the iron supports, moving from one to the other, spending a few minutes at each and concentrating on any spots where you get a bite. A hookless silver fly-spoon above the baited hook will invariably mean a better catch.

Rod bells are popular on piers, but except in the case of some flatfish, the fish will probably have been and gone by the time you reach your rod. If you do use one, then try to get a bell with a distinctive tone; as often, when a bell rings, all anglers within earshot rush to their rods hoping it was theirs— they must all patronise the same shop. When taking a rest, holding part of the line in hand is better than listening for bell-ringers.

Make a point of returning all small and undersize fish to the water at once, unharmed; they have no culinary value and ought not to 'do for the cat' or be left on the pier to die. And always be careful to remove all trace of your visit, before leaving the pier.

49

BEACH FISHING

As a preliminary, if possible, visit your chosen beach venue at low water to examine the ground for any gullies either running in from or parallel to the beach; also note any obstructions or rocky patches, and line up their positions so that you may avoid them when covered by the tide.

On arrival at the beach, the prevailing conditions are going to have a major influence on the choice of tackle assembly, and the following are among those to be taken into account.

Is the beach sandy, muddy, shingle or rocky, and is it a long shallowing out one, a gradual slope, or steep?

Is the state of the tide such that it will stream out your choice of end-tackle, or will it remain coiled in a heap just where it drops?

Is the weather calm, windy, or stormy, and is the surface flat or choppy, or perhaps with a swell or surf running in. Is the water itself clear or cloudy, and how far out is the deep water?

All these factors will have to be considered before you choose a suitable rod, according to whether a long or short cast is going to be necessary, and before you assemble your tackle. Choice of weights, again, will be determined by local conditions, and may be a torpedo type for casting, a bomb type for roving around over sand or shingle, or for fishing over snaggy or rocky terrain, any old expendable iron (nuts and bolts, etc), attached by lighter breaking-strain line.

The state of the tide will influence your choice of trace. In general, a single-hook trace is preferable, the longer the better, so that your bait can make a good traverse over a large area, and it is good practice to use some method of running gear, so that when a fish is mouthing the bait, or biting, before making off with it, he finds very little initial resistance. The use of more than one bait will tend to keep the trace on the bottom. All this, of course, assumes that there is sufficient current to swim the bait out. If there is not, your tackle is likely to bunch up in a useless heap and it will be wiser to use a paternoster.

When the sea is breaking heavily a long trace is more susceptible to snagging up and so a shorter trace is advisable with an additional hook mounted two feet or so above the lead. This can be very effective, especially over mud and sand, if cast well out and slowly retrieved to stir up the bottom occasionally as an attraction to the bait.

A light spiral weight is often a better alternative to a bomb weight when fishing over a shingle bottom as it is less liable to be impeded by the pebbles, and here a two-hook trace with two lively baits close together will set up good vibrations as the tide swishes it around. Avoid using too many swivels on this type of trace as they tend to make the baits plane about; a glass bead or a shot affixed near the end of the trace helps to prevent the hooks swinging back. And if you use a trace of lighter breaking strain than that of your reel line, fit a boom to help keep it clear when casting.

Many anglers prefer using a paternoster, either straight or as a running type, and both methods should be tried until sufficient experience has been gained to decide one's own preference under varying conditions.

When fishing over snaggy ground of any kind, a weight that is spoon- or kite-shaped will greatly help to plane it up when retrieving, and if crabs abound, try attaching small bottle corks to the trace, or else mount the trace on a boom two to three feet above your weight. But keep the trace short so that it swings clear of the bottom.

Early mornings and after dark are often the best periods of the day for success; especially if the tide is beginning to flood, bringing in the food for the smaller fish, who are in turn followed by the larger ones as the water deepens. The best times are usually about three hours before high water, and approximately three hours after it; though very often the first run of the ebb is also good.

A warm, stiff, on-shore wind with a rising tide is ideal, and where the scouring action takes place behind the breakers of the surf, that is the place to try your offerings, rather than a long cast further out. Use a single hook on a short trace if the sea is rough, as weed, surf, and scouring, will quickly tangle up a long flowing one.

It is seldom worthwhile fishing over a shingle beach when the water is quite clear, unless it is a shelving one or the water deepens suddenly, and if you want a really good sized fish, your chances will be greatly increased if you use a large bait. If you are using worms put on three or four, and whatever your bait, be generous.

DINGHY FISHING

In harbours, estuaries, and close inshore, dinghy fishing, as distinct from big-boat fishing well out to sea, can provide excellent sport, given the right tackle and conditions.

In April, as the sea temperature rises, the shallow creeks and upper reaches of harbours become the feeding grounds of the first arrivals, and it will pay off handsomely during the season if one learns all one can about one's chosen area by going afloat at a really low tide, taking a few soundings, noting all obstructions, and getting a mental picture of where the gullies branch out.

The dinghy angler, being mobile, can search around until he finds the feeding fish; usually they will first be found along the sides of the mudbank or 3 to 6ft from bottom, but as the water deepens with the rising tide they will start to spread out, some going off along the gullies while others, especially the bass, will congregate around any sunken obstructions and piles. The first batch to appear are usually the flounders, school bass, and eels, with the mullet coming along soon after, and by May there should be some plaice and pout around.

In shallow water of only a few fathoms, try to locate a good sandy patch amongst any rocky broken ground, and then anchor so as to fish over and around its edges, as this kind of spot is often very productive. Dinghy fishing, in which you are free to row or anchor at will, provides ample opportunity of trying out various kinds of end tackle, getting in some practice at float fishing and in the use of the baited spoon.

The weight used will depend on the run of the tide, but a spiral will be found as good as any, and if the run is strong then an anti-kink lead added before all will avoid twisting. If it is not a strong tide no weight may be needed, and a float and/or drift line will enable you to present a natural appearing bait.

At the top of the tide there usually comes a slack period when fish often seem to go off their feed, but, as it turns for the ebb and they vacate the shallows to return to the deeper channels, they all seem to feed with a bit more zest as they withdraw. A good plan at this time is to stream a drift line, or work a rubber eel or fly-spoon fairly deep as you keep the boat drifting a little slower than the tide by using a paddle or the oars, so that the bait streams out naturally.

When moving from place to place, a long trace with a rag-worm on a single hook, or a baited spoon, can be trolled (trailed) astern, with extra weight added, as you leisurely row along.

When the day is hot and rowing becomes hard work, or on other days when you wish to drop the anchor for a spell, the use of a rubby-dubby bag containing a mixture of any old stale bait, crabs, or food scraps can be useful. Tie it about 4ft from the anchor, to stream out particles under your boat in the hope of bringing the fish in your direction. In this case a simple drift line tackle should be set up by fixing a small swivel to the end of your reel line and connecting a long single hook trace so arranged as to swim around about 2ft off bottom.

If casting out and around, a second hook could be usefully employed to present a different type of bait; try using king rag for flounders and plaice, mud rag for shoal bass and mullet, herring strips for eels and pouting, and live sand-eels for the odd single bass roamer, and always try to keep the baits on the move.

Before setting out in your dinghy on any expedition, make sure that the 'bung', or drain plug is firmly shipped in its hole, and see that you have safety lanyards fitted to both your oars and the the rowlocks to prevent them being lost overboard.

NIGHT FISHING

Fishing after dark and on through the night to dawn can be very rewarding, for fish edge further into shallow water as soon as daylight begins to fail. The higher the tide the better, and should the full moon period and placid water coincide, then these are the most favourable conditions of all.

One of the main requirements is to be able to settle yourself quietly and above all, comfortably, so if possible procure a seat with a back rest, or a deck chair; folding stool seats are a poor substitute. Wrap up well, for even in summer the nights can get chilly; take plenty of drinks in flasks, and sandwiches for dawn, for hunger will bite even if fish don't.

You will need a good lamp, and one that can be fixed low with its beam parallel to the water is generally better than one pointing downwards or loosely flashing about. Alternatively, an electric headband lamp could be tried, if of sufficient illumination; it will leave both hands free and always point directionally where you look.

On arrival, set everything out to a plan so that all you will need is within easy reach, and nothing is likely to be knocked or kicked about if you have to make a sudden rush in the dark when your bell rings.

Whatever tackle you decide to use, a nylon line of heavier breaking strain than you would normally employ by day is advisable; it handles much better and will also instil greater confidence.

If casting out when it is very dark and you are unable to spot the tackle entering the water, a fixed-spool reel is the one to use. Most anglers take along a spare reel, or a spare spool, loaded and ready, for 'bird's nests' in the dark can be highly frustrating. Additional traces and baits should be to hand and, if anticipating conger, a long-handled gaff and a strong sack will be more than useful.

When darkness falls, the first to arrive will probably be the pouting, followed closely by pollack and whiting, all of whom feed very well at night, and then later come the bass. Night fishing for bass can often yield good results for they tend to forget much of their natural caution during darkness, and will take baits they would usually ignore during daylight. They will also take artificials much more readily; both 3in silver spoons and 4in Devon minnows have been reported as taking many a bass at night.

Pier anglers will find that flounders are often quite active at night, whilst legering with small hooks around the piles could find those tasty soles who do not roam very far from under the pier around the piles. Larger hooks adorned with fresh herring strips in the same area could connect with a good bass, but watch out for those underwater pier obstructions.

The beach angler will not need to make long casts once darkness has descended, as the fish will then be confident enough to seek their food quite close inshore. A large bait could attract a large fish if skate, conger, or bass are venturing in, whilst normal baits for flounders and others could be equally successful.

Boat anglers at night should remember the 'Rule of the Road' requirements and always have a white light ready for immediate display if other craft are in close proximity; an all-round visibility candle lantern is ideal as it can be placed on the floor boards to illuminate your gear inboard, or can easily be picked up to disclose your position if necessary. But try not to keep flashing it about or you may invite unnecessary rescue parties, or become a nuisance to navigation.

Night fishing can be a profitable sporting venture as a change and is well worth a trial, but, as with rock fishing, when the venue is off the beaten track, it is advisable that anglers should be accompanied by one or more rather than be alone.

DAWN FISHING

You are likely to find yourself cold and stiffish just before the dawn if you have been out all night fishing, but at the first streak you will need to be very much on the alert, for this is the hour when fish become really active and the big ones begin searching around. It is very easy to alarm fish in the early morning quietness, so if you are starting out early on a dinghy expedition, avoid noise as you near your venue by cutting the outboard and rowing quietly to your spot for the last hundred yards or so, and then, without splashing, quietly lower the anchor.

At the first light of dawn, the fish are likely to be found higher in the water than they usually are, until the day actually breaks, when they go down. Pollack will take a natural bait, whilst a fluorescent lure trolled quietly from a dinghy, or spinning from a jetty should make contact; they are often attracted by the red and white type of cellulose spinner, and by sunrise they will come to the usual feathers, rubber eels and other types of spinners, but by now they will be swimming deeper.

The use of a float at this hour will often provide some good sport if there are garfish about, as these then become extra lively and seem to jump and cavort about just for the fun of it. As the sun rises, the bass become exceedingly active, feeding voraciously, and a drift line offering a sand eel, or a legered squid or peeler, could meet with some success if they are about. And often at this time of day the beach angler may see shoals of mackerel venturing in very close when the tide is high. Spinning or light sliding float gear is then a good method of catching them.

If things are quiet on the bottom, with the fish being higher in the water than they usually are, a short spinning session can be tried until the day breaks, or perhaps a spot of float fishing.

ROCK FISHING

This is an entirely different pastime that holds quite a fascination for many anglers. The techniques employed will vary and, depending on the sea bed and topography in the vicinity, one may try float-fishing, spinning, or dropping a paternoster. In general, a long rod will be needed to reach out over rocks or water, and as getting snagged up between crevices is more than a possibility, use old iron or sandbag expendables; also take a gaff and net if you can.

The fish will be nosing around the weeds, so use shrimps or shellfish for bait, which is their natural food in this kind of locality. Use longish spinners or spoons, spin deep if you can, with plenty of sink and draw, and you may find feathers useful if there is room.

Some rock locations can be dangerous so always tell someone, preferably whoever will be expecting you on your return, where you are going. Wear suitable footwear for clambering over slippery footholds and see that your line of retreat is clear when climbing down, and make sure there is no possibility of being cut off by the tide. It is best not to go alone, especially in the dark, for should you slip and sustain an injury, aid may be impossible to obtain.

DRAGLINE FISHING

This is a dinghy pastime where one's tackle drags along on the bottom from a drifting dinghy. It is possible to cover a large area by this means but, of course, the sea bed should be a flat one with no obstructions.

CHAPTER 5

VARIATIONS OF ANGLING TECHNIQUES

Once the angler has become accustomed to the use of his tackle, and enjoyed several successful outings, he will be ready to experiment with some of the more interesting techniques adopted by sports fishermen who prefer to handle their rod instead of placing it in a rod rest or against a rail.

Spinning: The art of spinning is often neglected by sea anglers, possibly because they have not given it a fair trial, have been unlucky, or have not adopted the correct methods. Nevertheless, given plenty of patience and perseverance, it is good sport and if conditions are right, with the fish shoaling and feeding, or even when they are not about in large numbers, it often yields good results.

Spinning, as distinct from trolling, or whiffing behind a moving boat, is the ability to present and work an artificial bait, cast from any stationary stage or boat (anchored or drifting) in a natural manner; ie, to cast a light weight with the minimum of splash to alight just where you want it to, and then to work it so that it resembles a swimming, darting, or injured fish.

The ideal equipment would be a very light threadline outfit, comprising a 7 or 8ft light fibreglass or split-cane rod for casting, fitted with a light reel holding a fine line and carrying a very light weight. No weight will be necessary if the lure itself has sufficient built-in weight to make casting possible.

Use a line up to but not exceeding 10lb breaking strain if intending going deep, but to 6lb if keeping near the surface only.

The run of the tide will keep the lure off bottom and also

make it work; this is the most important part about spinning and you should be able to feel it working, continuously, right down to the rod handle. If it surfaces too quickly when it comes near you, this means it is riding too high, and you will need to add a little more weight to or near the anti-kink vane.

The speed of recovery is all important and has to be kept within fine limits all the time. If it is too fast, it will cause the lure to ride upwards; if it is too slow, or you halt its progress too long and thus allow it to sink, any fish considering a meal would have time to examine it, and finding the lure unpalatable, move off.

Ideally, retrieval should be made up of a variety of movements: quick, slow, up a bit, left to right, dodging here and there, down a bit, etc, all contributing towards an irregular pattern that keeps the lure moving and working all the time.

One is able to search at differing depths by changing weights, and this is well worth trying out at times, as mackerel and pollack near the surface are not the only fish taken by spinning. Many bottom feeders have also been taken on spinners worked well down.

If not using a revolving lure, an anti-kink weight will be necessary to prevent the lure from turning over, so select one best suited to the strength of the tide. Use a trace as long as you can manage, and a single hook is generally to be preferred, (but change to a treble if fish are biting well).

Natural baits for spinning are either sand-eels, squid, a bunch of two or three ragworms hooked lightly through the head, or a lask of mackerel; dead prawns or sand-eels can be tried but must be mounted so as to be presented correctly.

There are numerous artificial lures available in lieu of natural baits, and some of the self-weighted ones are most useful and can be cast well out without fitting extra lead higher up the trace. They are often weighted by adding small barrel weights on the bars of some spoons, or pellets fitted into the bodies of some of the fish-like lures.

Good artificial lures for spinning include rubber sand-eels, white wool tufts hiding a hook, or a silver tinsel-bound bunch of feathers, as well as the more common spinners, spoons, jiggers, etc. Any of these, or a small replica of a fish, a wobbling spoon with a squid tentacle, or any kind of fly-spoon will do the trick so long as it can be made to work continuously.

Most flashing lures will bring success, and from the many available to choose from in the shops, or to knock up at home, the mackerel spinner and/or the fly-spoon are considered by many anglers as being the best spinning lures invented, and are well worth trying out as a start. In recent years, too, much success has been obtained by the use of feathered lures, especially in camouflaging hooks.

When going after bigger fish, or if you have to cast some distance, eg, to reach out to a shoal, there is probably nothing better than the Devon-minnow type, which casts well because of its weight and is often taken as soon as it plops into the water.

If bass are seen chasing brit around near the surface, cast a fly-spoon above the feeding fish or to one side of them and try to bring the lure through the shoal. Pollack show little interest when following a bait until it is made to dart about, whereas mackerel seem to prefer the attraction of a steady slow flasher.

If going deep, use a small spoon on a short nylon length, about 6in, with a weight above the hook, commencing with 1oz about 18in up until you find the right solution. Cast as far out as possible, pause to let the lure sink, and then recover slowly and irregularly, pausing now and again so that the lead can scrape along the bottom.

A point to remember when spinning deep is that the reel line slants steeply towards the surface during any retrieving actions, as at (A), and this causes a heavily weighted lure to swim unnaturally. A lighter lure, with the lead well above the trace, as in (B), will enable it to work in the manner intended and remain correctly presented.

Of all the various artificials, the spoon-lure is probably the oldest, having been in use with very little change in design since fishing first began. When properly worked, it is as good as anything yet produced as a killer-bait, because not only does

Fig. 28   Spinning tackle

it spin, but it also wobbles and steers an erratic weaving course as the reel is slowly turned.

Let the spoon sink well down to commence with, then recover slowly by stirring up the bottom as it drags along a foot or two. Alternate this by working in 'sink and draw' fashion for a few turns and then stopping for a second or two, allowing the spoon to sink in a series of gyrating movements each time you pause, as it comes home. Never hurry the spoon through the water, but give the quarry plenty of time to take, as more fish are lost than gained because the bait has been moved too fast.

When a cast is fished out, do not snatch the spoon from the sea, but ease it up to the surface gently and you may find that pollack, bass, and mackerel will often follow it up undecidedly, finally taking it just as it is about to break surface.

Sea Fishing with a Float: In calm summer seas, floats can often be more successful than pater or leger; they permit you to fish at any required depth and will usually account for much better fish than other methods. With a float, you are able to fish your bait around over quite a large area, whilst the bottom fisherman usually leaves his where it pitches, often to garner crabs two or three at a time. Pier piles can also be fished much nearer and more systematically, and you can explore rocky and snaggy beds where the use of a leger or pater would be quite impracticable. June is regarded as the beginning of the float-fishing season, coinciding as it does with the annual inshore movement of garfish, pollack, mackerel, and bass.

A sea-float does not need to be very large, so start off with a medium-sized sliding float made from balsa or cork, as this will cast further than one of the hollow cellular type. The long ones are preferable to spherical ones as they offer less resistance to the fish when biting; and the buoyancy should only just be positive, thus helping to keep that resistance down. The float must be capable of taking sufficient weight to cast it a reasonable distance, preferably painted yellow so that it is easily visible up to fifty yards or so, and sufficiently sensitive to register the least nibble. At anything over that distance the length of line from rodtip to float will tend to deaden the effect of the strike and, as a general rule the nearer you fish your float within that distance the better. A good, light spinning rod and a reel holding a 10lb breaking-strain line is the ideal equipment, with a 3 to 4ft trace of 8lb breaking-strain attached to a suitable weight.

At the venue remember first to plumb the depth, and then attach your float to the reel line, putting a stopper above the float to keep the whole off bottom when streamed, (a rubber band is suitable for this). If not bottom fishing, then adjust the rubber band so that the tackle runs through the float and is stopped at the required depth when suspended.

The hooks are then baited-up according to which species may be about, or to any preference you may have. Usually, two hooks are sufficient—many anglers use only one—or another method is to use a four- or five-hook pater suspended on, or just off bottom to drift around. (See p. 65).

Sand-eels are a good bait generally, whilst shrimp, prawn, worms, peeler crab, whole whitebait, and fish strips are all very useful and should vary in size according to the hooks in use. From boats, the size of fish taken may vary in range from 1 to 10lb, according to the area, whereas from piers they usually run to a smaller average of 2lb.

If anticipating bass, place two or three shrimps or a lively prawn on a size 4 hook, or, if dead ones are used, on a size 2, and start your trial round about mid-water, taking into account that the warmer it is the nearer the surface the fish will be and that they tend to haunt any weed beds handy. Shoal, or 'school' bass, up to 2lb can be taken frequently, but large bass are lone fish and are not usually found among the small ones.

For pollack, bait up as for bass, or try a small ragworm, which is ideal for this species especially if a couple of small white beads are added over the eye of the hook. Give the bait some movement, gently retrieving a few yards followed by a short pause, so that the bait flutters up and down as the line slides to and fro through the float.

For mackerel and garfish, who are mainly interested in fish or worm baits, an added attraction will be silver paper wrapping round the shank of the hook. At dawn and sundown, these fish may be close to the surface, but in daytime they are mostly a few fathoms down.

Bream fishing with a float is a particularly enjoyable method of angling. With a light float and single hook to a trace, use sufficient weight to keep about 3ft off the bottom; float a small worm or oily fish strip bait away a short distance, and then sink and draw to ascertain the depth at which they are feeding and vary your direction and distance at will. Flounders and mullet also offer good prospects from floats, whilst wrasse can be taken with them around piers and other rocky terrain.

When float fishing, the angler holds his rod and should keep an almost constant watch on his float so as not to miss the slightest nibble through sight or touch. It is an ideal method of searching a large area at different depths, but if you slacken your vigil by standing the rod against the railings you will almost certainly miss striking when the float dips.

Shore fishermen can also fish with a float, and when bass are feeding near the surface, a suspended tackle will usually take more fish than legering, so try a bubble float to aid the cast, or improvise with an assembly adapting a sponge-rubber ball with a small plastic tube, such as in a ballpoint pen, as a means of swimming your offering below the surface at any desired depth. Obviously, in any such rig the float will not serve as a bite detector.

Add a hook to the line, attach a spiral about a foot above it, and then fix a stopper (which must be able to pass through the rod rings, but stops at the float) to determine your depth. The weight will help the trace to avoid curling back when cast, and a gentle cast should enable you to place the float fairly well out.

The following diagrams show the orthodox ways of using some of the types of floats that most sea anglers prefer; few are alike but all work in a similar manner, whatever their shape, size, colours, or material construction.

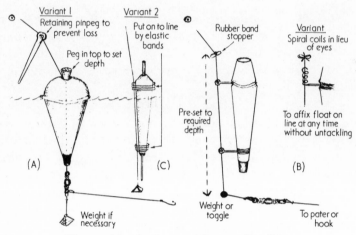

Fig. 29   Two basic types of sea-angling floats

The two basic types, shown above, are the fixed (or adjustable) float, (A) which moves together with the line, and the sliding float (B), to which the line is attached and yet allowed to move independently.

The fixed float is ideal for general use, especially in waters where the depth is less than the rod length; it is ideal for flounder spoons, and suitable for minor adaptations, quick changing of weights as the tide varies, or unpegging to alter line length, etc. It is not essential to thread the line through the float as in (A) and the float may be attached at any point using rubber bands, (C). Remember, though, that if the peg is set in for any great depth, when reeling in the float will come to the rod tip while the fish is still in the water, and may not lift clear. This may be overcome, and greater depths used for stopping, by avoiding the peg type and using a slender long type which can be attached where it is wanted by rubber bands

(C), in which case as the float nears the rodtip it is simply removed from the rubber bands entirely and the fish reeled in normally. By discarding the peg, the fixed can be used as a 'slider'.

The sliding float is usually preferred for its versatility in that it can be adjusted to keep the weight off rocky bottoms, or to any depth just below the surface. The rubber band or nylon stopper when fitted must be thin enough to pass through the rod rings, but not through the float ring, eyes, or any spiral being used. The line may be rove direct through the centre, or through outrigger eyes or spirals, as shewn.

These two basic types have been modified and varied in many ways, but the general principle is easily understood, and usually applies.

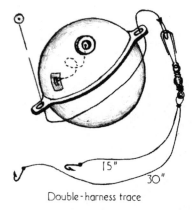

Double-harness trace   Fig. 30 A bubble float

A third type of float, the bubble float, is now seldom seen but it has its advantage in that it may be filled, or partly filled with water to serve also as a weight for casting in lieu of lead. Rigged out as shown, using a twin trace, it is a boon for casting a float a considerable distance off shore.

A popular practice, especially when crabs are prevalent, is to stream a paternoster below a float (A), so weighted that it will bounce and wander with the baits, fluttering out from a vertical suspension below a float, which is itself often submerged and used as the suspender and not as a bite detector.

Frequent stopping and releasing the reel line in a tideway will attract attention as you control it up or down, near or far. This practice is referred to as the 'sunken float' method, or if so weighted as to be kept in a certain position, it is termed 'stationary tackle'. A trace (B) may be substituted for the paternoster, and it is easy to change to a drift-line by detaching the trace at 'X', removing both float and weight, and rebuckling your line to the trace to fish higher.

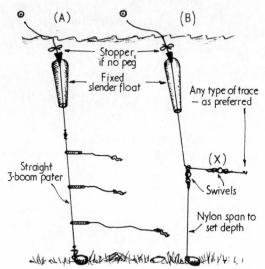

Fig. 31
Fishing a sunken float

Another method, very good for shallow water casting, especially when night fishing, is shown, where a bite is felt on the main line. The weight can be slid up to the float, and so travels first on casting. A foul hook by the trace is unlikely when casting and a very efficient strike can be made. It is also easy to change to a leger simply by removing the float, which is not on the reel line but on a short separate 2 to 4ft length, and securing the weight.

If you are fishing with your tackle away down on the bottom and bites are scarce, a novel method is to try a spot of float fishing at the same time, without rigging up another rod.

A float, weight curl, 4 to 6ft of nylon are assembled as shown

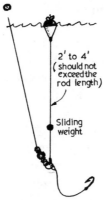

Fig. 32   A shallow water float

below, clipped on to the line and lowered down to the surface to stream out, allowing sufficient length to ensure that it will shake out clear. The peculiar effect of a bite swimming up and down the line is worth the slight tangle of two sets of tackle when you bring it in.

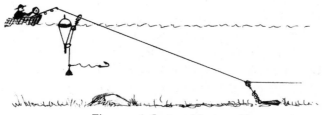

Fig. 33   A float and leger tackle

Drift Lining: This method of fishing is simply what the name implies, ie, allowing a line to drift with the tide without using a float. It may be used to swim your light end-tackle near the surface or at any desired depth, the position being controlled by selection of a weight suitable to combat the strength of the tide.

Very often just a hook to the line will suffice if the bait will submerge, or a spiral lead can easily be fitted to swim it down where required. An anti-kink lead will be needed for those baits which tend to swivel about. Once your tackle is streaming

67

clear, your line can be 'thumbed off' the reel to any distance required, and this method will be found most useful from pier, jetty, or dinghy wherever there is a tidal run.

Some anglers find it rewarding to first stream their line out a good distance, and then clip their weight on and send it down by gradual shakes of the rod, thus exploring the varying depths. A nylon paternoster can also be used if it is preferred to a single hook but in all forms of drift lining you will need to hold your rod and be able to feel the bites direct, rather than placing the rod down once the line is out.

Trolling: This method differs from drift lining in that it is carried out from a moving boat, with the tackle and bait trailed astern at any desired speed and depth. If your dinghy is moving slowly, a light lead may take the bait down and keep it at the required level, but if the speed is increased, or the tidal current runs stronger, a heavier lead will become necessary to prevent the tackle rising too near the surface. Similarly, the greater the speed, the longer will be the length of line needed and the heavier the weight to get the bait down and keep it there.

In deep trolling the deeper you go the slower should be your speed and if the tide is really strong and the water quite deep, you may find it difficult to maintain the desired depth. If so, this problem can be overcome with the aid of a companion to act as helper and a heavy sinker of say 10 to 20lb.

Secure the sinker to a fairly strong rope(B); and attach one end of a connecting line (D) of any ordinary light line to the weight. The other end of the line is connected to a breaking line (C), which could be a 3in or so length of weak cotton or yarn; the free end of the breaking line is now secured to the fore end of your tackle at the buckle where it joins the fishing line (A) from the reel.

When a fish strikes, your tackle should detach and free the sinker as the weak spot breaks (C). The weight can then be hauled up out of the way—which is where the helper comes in—leaving you with a fish on and no sinker. When using this method from an anchored dinghy in deep waters and a strong

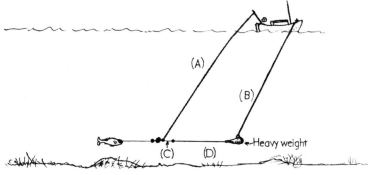

Fig. 34   Deep trolling from a small boat

tide, use only sufficient weight to hold the bottom. The connecting line (D) can, of course, be attached to the lowering line (B) to any required depth.

If at any time you run out of bait, the nose-weighted feathered lure illustrated below and representing a squid can be trolled very effectively. It can easily be knocked up at home ready for such an occasion and white wool can be used successfully if no feathers are available.

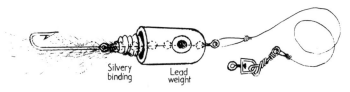

Fig. 35   Artificial squid lure for trolling

Whiffing: This popular pastime consists of trailing a baited hand-line from the stern of a slowly moving boat. Extra attraction is often obtained by suddenly whiffing in a yard or so of line and then quickly reverting to normal, to vary the flash and speed. Used with feathers, it is an excellent way to take mackerel.

The Sink and Draw Method: It often pays to move your bait around an area and search different places, rather than staying in one place, and the sink and draw technique is ideal for this purpose, especially when moving along a pier. A long rod is to be preferred and the idea is to simulate an injured fish by working the rod so that the bait will rise and fall continuously in a series of jerks at short intervals.

Fig. 36   The sink and draw method

A fold-over or anti-kink lead, sufficient to take the bait down and swim it head first, is attached just above the swivel, on the reel line, and the normal trace should be about 18 to 24in in length for good results.

This method is also often employed when float fishing, the line being drawn through the float for just a few feet and then released to flutter out the lures, thus giving slight variations of depth. If the lure used is a small fish, it will appear wounded and an easy prey as it makes its erratic swim and will prove particularly attractive to fish that prefer a moving bait.

CHAPTER 6

NATURAL BAITS

Many types of baits are used to attract fish to the hook; they vary from place to place, with different methods of fishing, and according to anglers' preferences, but the following points are generally worth bearing in mind:

Use live baits if they are obtainable, as you will then be more than halfway to success.

If you order bait for delivery, open it immediately it arrives.

Never put live bait in tins, and do not carry bait tightly packed in small containers.

Correct presentation of the bait is all important for successful angling.

Use smaller baits in very clear water, and larger ones where the water is dirty or clouded.

Pieces of fish strip looking the worse for wear are not worth using.

For convenience in listing and studying them, baits may be said to fall into four separate categories:

(1) Live baits. Any living species such as small fish, or prawns, shrimps, sand-eels, as well as worms.

(2) Fish baits. Dead mackerel, herring, or any other fish, either whole, in strips or sections.

(3) Shell fish. Crabs, limpets, mussels, cockles, etc.

(4) Artificials. All types of spinners, spoons and lures.

Incidentally, garden worms and snails are of little use in salt water as they will quickly die, but they are sometimes worth trying out in estuaries.

The use of frozen or preserved baits is a matter of personal preference; sand-eel, herring, whitebait, etc, kept frozen until required for use, can be excellent baits, but with those which have merely been salted down much will depend on how the salting was done and how long they have been kept. Many such kinds of bait may be bought in a preserved state, but all should be thoroughly washed before use.

Pilchard or anchovy oil is considered by many anglers to give an added flavour to these and some other baits, but remember that very little oil is required and keep it well away from your other gear as the smell persists for a long time.

Correct baiting is one of the main arts of fishing, so never be diffident about changing from one to another, and if, on occasion, none of the usual baits is procurable, remember that fresh or fried sausage, tripe, fat meat, bacon, herring roe, bananas and many other such food items have all accounted for good fish.

LIVE BAITS

Sand-eels, (or Launces): Two varieties are common to British waters, the Greater with an average length of 8 to 12in, and the Lesser, which averages 4 to 6in.

The Greater is green above and paler below, with silver bands on its sides, whilst the Lesser is of a more overall silvery colour. They both live in the shallows and may be found burrowing in the sand at low water, especially at spring tides, or swimming at or near the surface in large shoals. They are often quite difficult to locate and catch, and to keep alive for any length of time.

Special small-mesh nets were once popular for gathering them, but the tendency nowadays is to dig or rake over the sand at low-tide mark with a special reaping-hook type of scraper with a handle. The top three inches of sand is scraped over with one hand into the other hand, held as a scoop under the water ready to trap and catch any eel that may be dragged out of the sand. You need to act quickly immediately you spot one, and a piece of prawn net on the rake will help to prevent their escape. Hard, dry sand can also be scraped over, but here you will need to be extra quick to stop them burying themselves to elude you. And at all times, watch out for the poisonous weever which also buries into the sand.

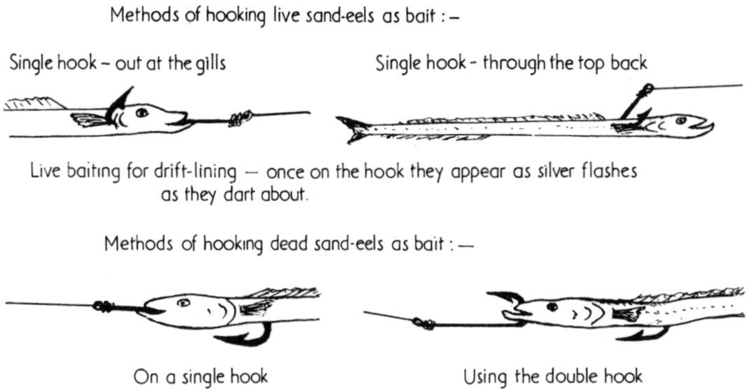

Methods of hooking live sand-eels as bait : –

Single hook – out at the gills

Single hook – through the top back

Live baiting for drift-lining — once on the hook they appear as silver flashes as they dart about.

Methods of hooking dead sand-eels as bait : —

On a single hook

Using the double hook

Figs. 37 and 38   Baiting with sand eels

Sand-eels are extremely fragile creatures to be treated carefully at all times, and to keep them alive it is customary to transfer them to a wooden box, or 'courge', which is always kept submerged. When dinghy fishing, this box is generally hung over the stern, so that when the eel is selected it is put on the hook under water, and the tackle lowered to prevent the eel from breaking surface. They are of little or no use when so damaged as to appear unnatural.

Prawns and Shrimps: These are two distinct species, the prawn being distinguishable by an unmistakeable spear projecting from the head, which is absent in shrimps. The prawn is always a transparent yellow, whilst shrimps are of a greyish colour, though they often camouflage themselves when over mud. Prawns are usually found close to seaweed or rocks, or around the piles, whilst shrimps prefer sand or mud.

Suitably baited nets can be put down in likely places to catch them, and for the popular bagnet method you will require a small-mesh net about 15 to 20in in depth, attached to the rim forming the mouth of the net. The rim should be of reasonably large diameter, say approximately 2ft, (an old cycle wheel is frequently used), and the whole of the 'drop' is bridled and secured to a well corked rope.

73

Stale fish is quite a good bait, though fresh fish pieces will also be taken, and kipper is often an attraction. Cod's head and skate offal are good, and ideal if edible crabs or lobsters are in the area. Note that if dropping your gear for lobsters only, then a 1in or so mesh net could be substituted for the small one. Secure your bait in the centre of the net so that the tide will not move it away, and the rim dropped around it will encircle it with any visitors when hoisted.

The net should be dropped gently down in any likely position, such as from a pier or jetty, and left undisturbed for some time. For recovery and examination, a smooth, quick, continuous pull is best. The most profitable time is when darkness falls, especially when the sea is calm and they seem to feed best at low water. October is considered as being the middle of the season.

Prawn pots are very often set from boats, especially where there are quiet patches in harbours, or long stretches in small bays where a 'fleet' of pots can be put down, strung out as a 'trot' and each one identifiable by a small marker buoy. All gear should be hauled in at sunrise or soon after, and once your haul is gathered, it will keep best when stowed with wet seaweed.

On rocky coasts prawns and shrimps often become trapped in some of the many small pools as the tide recedes, when they may be easily scooped up by the use of a small net, but these are usually small ones. Both are ideal baits when live, but are also quite useful when dead, the dead ones being more attractive as bait when unboiled.

Fig. 39   Correct methods of baiting prawns when alive (left) and when dead

Worms: There are two main species, Ragworm and Lugworm, both of which have for long been traditional baits. Of the two, lugworms are the least difficult to obtain by digging, and are less expensive to buy, supplies being plentiful at most angling resorts.

The lug is at home on many sandy beaches, where it prefers the area just above low-water mark, and a lug-infested beach will be found to be covered with small spiral sandy casts and round depressions. On such a beach, and armed with a long-pronged fork, the procedure is to locate one of the many casts, which will indicate that the tail of the worm is somewhere below that spot. But do not dig right there for, as it is the head that does the boring through the sand, the worm may be some inches away, and if you dig at that mark it will vacate its danger spot in a very few seconds.

Look around, and about 9in from the cast you should find a small conical depression in the sand, an inch or so in diameter, which is the worm's breathing hole. The head of the worm is situated about six inches below that, and the worm itself has found its abode by lying almost parallel to the surface about six inches below it, in a direction between the cast and the depression.

Prod your fork into the sand a few inches from the depression, dig down about a foot, then work the fork round to the cast, when you should be able to lift it undamaged if you are careful to grasp it amidships. If you try to pull it by the tail end only, that is all you will be left with.

If there are casts there are worms and if they appear plentiful it will pay you to dig trenchwise over any of the likely spots. When caught, keep them in a deep wooden box containing plenty of coarse sand covered with a good layer of wet seaweed. Soft sand will tend to suffocate them and do not overcrowd the box. Kept in the dark in a cool place, they will remain fresh for a few days, less in warmer weather, and should be inspected daily. Use a flat shallow box to transport them on your expeditions, and do not mix them with ragworms.

Ragworms delight in living in mud or a combination of mud and sand, and the more evil-smelling it is the more they seem to thrive in it. The black mud sometimes found in harbours and estuaries at low water is good hunting ground, though they may also be found in gravelly sand. 'Rags' come in a variety of sizes from the large king-rag (over a foot long), the ordinary mud-rag, the harbour or jumper-rag, to the smaller red and white rags, which are only from 1 to 3in long.

Try and discover where their beds are rather than seeking out the odd one, as this will save a lot of back-breaking work as well as time. It is usually easy to spot where a rag has burrowed down into the mud or sand as the tunnel entrance remains; there are no casts or depressions, and they usually lie somewhere near the entrance, rarely more than six inches below. One could also turn over small rocks and mudweed and search under these, for many of the smaller ones, which make good bass baits, do not bother about burrowing but just seek a hide-out.

As with lug, do not pull them from their run as they easily break off, and when handling one, beware of its pincer nippers, which can give you a surprising but quite harmless bite. Ragworms may be kept for several days if spread out on some sacking or a newspaper in grit, coarse sand, or vermiculite; they should be kept dry and cool, looked at daily, and any deteriorating ones, together with any rotting wet newspaper, removed.

Both kinds of worm will quickly perish if contaminated with fresh water or exposed to heat. Tins and galvanised containers should never be used and a wet seaweed covering at all times will help a lot. When digging for rag, you may turn up a large dark-coloured lug; this is called the black lug and is an excellent bait. Whelk shells, often taken over by hermit crabs, are also worth breaking open, for these may reveal a red-brown rag deep within the spiral.

The methods of baiting up the worms on the hooks vary quite a bit according to different localities and personal preferences, but bear in mind that the hook point must be always left 'in the clear' (uncovered). The head of the worm should be permitted to hang from the hook as fish are most interested in the juicy head of any worm, the tail usually being filled with sand. Flatfish sucking in a worm tail-first will often reject it altogether, so it could be to advantage to pinch some of the tail off when baiting the hook.

Different ways of presenting rag and lugworms on the hook:

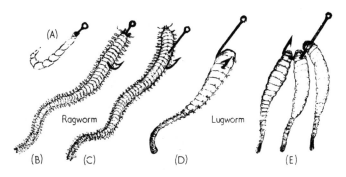

Fig. 40   Five methods of baiting with rag and lugworm

(A) Covering the whole hook, this being the method used for small whites and reds, or, for economy, a section of a large rag.

(B) Threading the whole hook, by penetration at the mouth and sliding the head up the hook shank as far as possible, bringing the point out clear.

(C) Somewhat similar to (B), except that the hook is entered at a point where the ragworm's head may be left hanging free to move. The puncture should be carefully made to retain the contents.

(D) is a single lugworm, which can be put on a hook in several ways; many use the threading process as in (B), others anchor the hook by entering it at the hard tail, bringing it out again and on through the head.

(E) Here a bunch of worms is lightly threaded through the head and allowed to hang loosely. They may also be hooked on as at (C), slid up the line until all are hooked, and then brought down on top of each other to form a large cluster.

Very small fish are sometimes used whole as a live bait, pouting being the usual choice for this purpose. A very young fish, 3 to 5in long, is ideal on a 3ft trace with a 3oz weight, and will be found to make a very good swim for bass, starting about 4ft up from the bottom. A fairly large hook is used, inserted either through the shoulder or lip so that the fish can still dart about. This method is sometimes used by off-shore fishermen after tope and other large fish, but can be useful in harbours at times.

Herring, mackerel, and many other species of fish in fresh condition, or even kipper and bloater, all provide suitable fish baits, used either in sections or cut into strips, whilst cuttlefish, squid, sprats, sand-eels, etc can add to the menu.

When a small whole fish is used, it should be presented to be swallowed head first. If using a single hook, it should be size 1 or larger and inserted near the tail to protrude from the belly. Using two hooks, both size 4, one is arranged to come out at the gills, and the other about halfway down the opposite side, both being bound to the fish at the tail if not threaded through the fish by a baiting needle.

Half a fish is the bait for very large fish only, and if you kipper a fish for this purpose, leave a half tail on each side, and puncture a few small gaps in the side to allow some oily juices to run from the body. Put the hook in the tail end, right through and out clear, when the tail end itself can be bound to the hook eye with fine wire (fuse wire is ideal for this); when swallowed, the hook will not be so deep down.

The two most important points to remember when using any type of fish bait are to ensure the barb is clear to ensure penetration, and to examine them frequently and renew them once they become scraggy looking.

The method of preparing all the popular fish baits for the hook, in sections or strips, is straightforward. First obtain a special baitboard to work on, and retain it as part of your tackle. Then, with a sharp knife, remove the head, all fins, and clean off the scales. Next, kipper, slit, and bone the fish, and lay it on the board skin side down. Now cut it diagonally into strips, each up to 1in wide, as (A), slice off any excess flesh if too thick, neatly trim each piece, and transfer each cutting to a small box.

For use, select a bait in proportion to the size of your hook; insert the hook in the fleshy side and bring it back through the thinner light skin, as (B), then trim the trailing corners to make it somewhat fish-shape, taking care that the barb is not hidden.

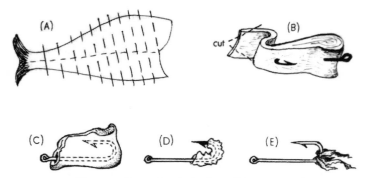

Fig. 41   Preparing baits from fish cuttings

Beware of two common faults when baiting up with fish strips. One is using a bait much too large, as (C), with the hook hidden, as the penetration can be doubtful and some fish will be scared of it. The other is using a bait too small, as (D), which the small fry will nibble at and the larger fish ignore. The bedraggled example as (E) is useless and should speedily be renewed.

To cut out a mackerel 'lask' or 'last'; cut a piece of the skin near the tail as shown, from 2 to 3in long, with a pattern of one-third dark top and two -thirds predominating silver belly area. A similar one can, of course, be cut from the other side. Hook it on by the narrow end, leaving the hook shank clear, or if the hook is a large one then twist after the first insertion and hook again, and let it hang from the hook as shown. If spinning, the flesh should first be removed from the skin.

Fig. 42   Preparing a mackerel lask

Other Fish Baits: Cuttle and squid: These peculiar-shaped creatures, with their tentacles, are good bait and can often be found during the summer months, sometimes swimming just under the surface. When dinghy fishing, especially over sandy areas, any piece of pouting or other unwanted fish will often attract these creatures if secured to a light line, lightly weighted and lowered to the bottom. Raise your bait almost to the surface from time to time and you may find that it has been securely grasped by either a cuttlefish or squid, a crab or even a lobster or whelk.

The tenacity of these creatures when dinner is in their hands is such that they will not release their hold until they suddenly realise they may be breaking surface, so if you want whatever is clinging there, get your landing net quickly into the water and below your bait. Do not lift it out until you are sure what is there, and if it should be a squid, keep it under water until it has expended its ink-sac, whose contents can otherwise cause a nasty mess over you or your dinghy. A very small squid on a large hook is almost a certainty if large bass are in the vicinity, whilst the larger sizes will cut up into several tentacles to use singly, and many strips cut about 4in by 1in. These baits are extremely tough and will remain on the hook a long time.

Sprats: This natural bait may be netted in the autumn through to the winter months in some coastal areas, or is available from fishmongers during this period. Shop-bought sprats however, after all their packing, travelling, and usage, quickly tend to go soft and can damage easily, so handle them carefully.

When used whole, they are a first-rate bait for bass, turbot, skate, conger, and whiting. Some anglers prefer removing the head and/or tail, and they can be halved or divided into cutlets if in short supply. For beach casting it can be advantageous to tie the whole fish on to the hook with a little wool or fine wire.

Sprats may be preserved quite easily, and will keep until the following season if carefully processed. In February or March, obtain a few over the required quantity, wash them thoroughly in cold water, check them well over and discard the imperfect.

Then immerse them in a dish containing a 75 per cent solution of formalin and keep them covered for 48 hrs as a toughening-up process. The final stage is to put them into glass jars with their heads downwards, (a 1lb screw-top jam jar is ideal for this purpose), and to cover them with a solution that is half glycerine and half water.

Skate Liver: The liver discarded when winging a skate is a really deadly bait to take bass and grey mullet, or sometimes bream, but owing to its very soft composition it is only suitable for use when one can gently lower it to stream away slowly.

SHELLFISH BAITS

Several crustacean baits are available and all varieties are fairly easy to obtain. First and foremost are the common scourges of the sea bed, the crabs which so persistently rob your baits, but as a few of them can be useful as bait, some knowledge of their many differences may be helpful. It is in the early spring, as the water begins to warm up, that crabs make their way to the rocky areas, where they seek a refuge in which to shed their shells and to mate.

The Hardback Crab: This type, of which there seems to be a preponderance whenever you fish, is of practically no use as a bait, unless a small quantity of the younger ones can be gathered up and immersed in glycerine to soften them. After a time they will become sufficiently soft to use as a bait, when a good wash with sea water followed by a smear of pilchard oil will produce a suitable offering, but they are seldom used thus nowadays.

The Softback Crab: This type is distinguishable solely by feeling it, for it is at that stage of life when the old shell has been shed and the new one has not yet completed its hardening-off process. The body may be heavily wrinkled as the shell is forming up, the claws will be small and at this stage they make good bait.

The Peeler Crab: This description is applied to the crab when it is in the process of shedding its shell in order to grow larger, and a new soft shell is waiting within to expand and harden once the old shell has been shed. When this occurs and the new soft one appears, they are termed 'jellies', and when the new one begins to show signs of hardening, they are transformed into 'crispies', eventually to become a softback until fully hardened-off.

Crabs grow out of their shells and cast them periodically, and during this process, all peelers are considered ideal baits. All traces of the old shell should first be removed and they will be found most effective on the bottom. The jellies, too, are superb bait to use when float fishing, whilst crispies are suitable for use at any depths and with any method.

The popular way to present a crab bait, up to the size of a florin is shown here, used whole, but when mounting larger ones replace the hook with a treble, right through the centre, and wrap wool or a hairnet to bunch it together. Alternatively, remove the stomach flap, legs, and claws and hook through the middle leg socket, or through the stomach flap and back, or any other way you think presentable.

Fig. 43   Hook bait with crab

The best time to collect crabs is at low water of a good spring tide. Search any area of weed-covered rocks, clusters of bladder wrack beds, and similar growths, and work from low back to the half-tide mark. It is advisable to wear gloves on your quest, as many of the rocks may be barnacle encrusted or jagged, and remember that the safe and easy way of grasping your crab is to hold it between the thumb and index finger, which are placed on the rim of the shell behind its two largest claws.

Both peelers and softbacks are often carried on the backs of some of the larger crabs for protection, so keep a weather eye open for a large unwanted one scurrying away in case he may have a passenger for you. To keep crabs, place them in a box filled with wet seaweed or wrack.

The Hermit Crab: This small curled-up variety makes his abode within the shell of a whelk, though there are some with their own shell that somewhat resemble a snail. They are one of the best baits obtainable and may be caught by a baited drop-net, or by lowering the weighted baited line, as for cuttle and squid, leaving it on the bottom for a short while and then hopefully bringing it to the surface. But have your landing net handy as they sense danger and will often release the bait before reaching the surface.

Fig. 44   Baiting a hermit crab

The usual way of using it to bait-up is as shown here, but if it is a fair sized one it may be divided up to leave a tentacle on each piece; keep the tail separate as this is the best portion.

The Spider Crab: This type can be a nuisance on many good fishing spots, and where they do occur there are usually hundreds in the vicinity. It is comparatively large and with its claws wrapped around it is circular in appearance, but has no value as bait.

Crab baits are not generally sought for by anglers, possibly perhaps because of the trouble in getting suitable ones, but they do make ideal bait just after dawn in early summer. In general, they often produce a good fish over low-lying stony terrain, but are not so successful on sandy shores. Even so, do not disdain their use if at any time a useful one comes your way.

Slipper Limpets: These shellfish will cling together in small clumps, usually being attached to brown ribbon weed; each nestles on its neighbour and, when separated, their shape does bear some resemblance to a slipper.

They are a greyish brown outside, while the inside, which contains the delicate fish, is a pale pink. They are often to be found washed up on the beach after a storm and are considered a superior bait for a bass, being his natural food in the areas where they abound.

To separate and prise apart each shell from the other, use a flat knife, which is also useful for freeing and extracting the limpet carefully. Put your hook through the middle of the round yellow centrepiece, and two or three may be used on one hook provided they are not jammed into a messy heap which will affect your strike.

Limpets: The ordinary type of limpet differs from the slipper in being oval in shape, with its shell conically flattened out. They may be seen adhering to the surface of rocks, and although possessing great adhesive powers, a hard tap on the side of the shell will usually dislodge them, when they become easy to extract.

Pass the hook through the soft part first, and then right through the whole, using two if the hook is large. They are a suitable bait for bream, pouting, and whiting, whilst any hungry bass or pollack might take them, but, in general, they are not highly rated as bait.

Razor Fish: These are sand-loving shellfish somewhat resembling the old type 'cut-throat' razor, from which they derive their name. They are usually about 4in long, and may be discovered near or beyond the low-water mark on shelving sand or muddy sandy areas.

They may be gathered by digging, but tread very lightly, for if you disturb them unduly they will soon take alarm and bury themselves a couple of feet down. Look for the big circular depression in the sand, and close by you will observe a key-top shaped shallow depression recently formed; then insert the tines of your fork about 3in from the key-top sign which is just over the razor fish and dig down, deep if necessary. Leave on any wet sand adhering, for moisture, and place the fish in a wooden box. Another method sometimes employed is to drop common salt slowly into the burrow hole to make them rise. They are fairly easy to open, and make a splendid bait for bass, etc.

Limpets, on rocks   Slippers, on beach   Razors, in sand

Fig. 45   Limpets, slippers and razor fish are all suitable baits

Mussels: These are one of the best of all shell fish for general use and have accounted for many specimen fish. Almost all fish will take them, with one fortunate exception of the unwanted dogfish.

Choose the larger ones only, and to open them (using a non-folding knife not a clasp knife;) slide one shell-side a little to enable you cut into the join, and then sever the hinge muscle and open it. Push the hook through the yellow brown heart, or tongue, from side to side, and then on to the cut muscle. Mussels will keep up to a fortnight or so immersed in salt water, which should be changed every few days.

Whelks: A hammer is needed to open the shell; they are tough on hooks, and a fine bait for cod, but most other fish are not interested. One advantage is that crabs cannot remove them as easily as they strip other baits.

Cockles: These lie just under the sand and are disclosed by small holes. They are rated as poor bait in most areas, but cod, pout, and flatfish will often take them.

Clams: These will also be found in the sand, but well down, and are somewhat similar to the cockle; very few fish will be attracted by them.

Winkles: These are very small and tender to use as a bait, for not only are they messy, but several will be required for one hook. They are, however, a fair bait for mullet, whilst whiting, cod, and a few other species sometimes find them worth trying.

Oysters: Being a table delicacy, these will obviously not be used as a bait, neither will they come within the range of capture by the average angler. But there is one part of an oyster, known as the 'beard' which is inedible and if you can obtain some of these from an oyster stall holder, they are one of the finest bass baits procurable.

CHAPTER 7

ARTIFICIAL BAITS

These include all types of attractions made from various materials, and may be subdivided into three classes:
  (a) Facsimiles of living creatures, ie, imitations of fish, worms, crabs, etc, (fish being much superior, and crabs usually disappointing).
  (b) Lures that are intended to represent (a) when moving, such as plastic strips for sand-eels, feathers, etc, or any other simulation.
  (c) All those attractions that have no resemblance to living creatures, but are used as a magnet to draw fish near to a bait. These include all spinners, spoons, and flashers.
  Let us examine them in that order, illustrating the most popular ones and noting their distinctive behaviour in use.
  The Rubber Sand-eel: This is a very popular sea-fishing lure, and can be made in a few minutes from a length of small diameter rubber tubing, a length of rigid brass wire, a swivel, and a ringed hook about size 4; (a ready-made material ideally suited to the purpose is the ordinary common rubber draught excluder). The eels may be made to any length, and as the average is about 6in, cut this length from the tubing and trim off the edging as shown to represent the fairly long dorsal fin. Now cut the two ends, one with a V-shape to make a realistic mouth and the other to represent the tail.
  To make the backbone, take a length of the brass wire and secure one end of it to the hook-eye. Then measure it along the rubber to the mouth, with the swivel body wholly enclosed in the mouth and the hook shank laid within the body. Determine the length where the swivel is to be connected and when the

parts are ready for assembly thread the wire, bind the mouth neatly to resemble gill covers whilst holding the swivel, and add a pair of eyes if you wish.

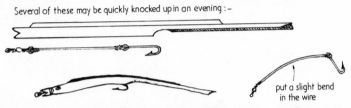

Fig. 46   How to make an imitation sand-eel

The wire must now be carefully bent to produce the wriggling movement without which the eel would lose its attraction as a bait. It may need to be adjusted to ensure it wriggles and darts about, and if it turns and rolls around instead of moving from side to side, an anti-kink lead above it may be called for.

These eels may be coloured to choice, and when satisfactorily completed should be carefully stowed in a stiff container together, as any further bending after trials will adversely affect their performance. In strong tides, an anti-kink could be essential to stop the eel spinning about unnaturally, whilst in deep water a spiral may be called for just above the swivel. Remember to fit a hook proportionate to the size of the eel.

Imitation Fish: There are numerous types of these available from any tackle dealer, and many patterns for the 'do-it-yourself' man to work from; they are comprehensively called 'plugs'.

Plugs are to a large extent made of wood, but some are of light metal or plastic material; they may be solid or hollow, floaters or sinkers, all in one piece or joined, self-weighted, or fitted with a diving vane.

They can be expensive, but if you can whittle a piece of wood, you can make one yourself for only a few pence. Look around for old dowel rod, paint brush handles, or other close-grain wood of similar shape, and when making the body, do not saw off a length but do the necessary whittling and smoothing on the end of the handle, where it will be easier to shape up. The two halves may be made as one or cut separately and trimmed afterwards. The two cut-away areas on the sides of the front piece allow the water pressure to act on the wall face of the rear section, and this, through the action of the diving vane, will give the lure its attraction by enabling the tail to wobble from side to side, making it lifelike.

One most important point is to ensure that the plug is properly balanced centrally on its underside so that it fishes the right way up and on an even keel. Any weight to be added must be fitted to the front section, for if added to the rear it will destroy the required wriggle and also tend to make it fish on its tail, and so look lifeless. Weights on the back will make it top heavy, and thus unbalanced it will fish upside down.

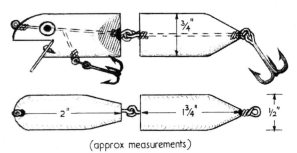

(approx measurements)

Fig. 47   Details of an effective plug bait

To add weight, use small lead shot inserted in small holes drilled in the belly of the fish, and seal with plastic wood. To find the amount to use, test in a basin, not forgetting that salt water is more buoyant than fresh water, and that the object is just to overcome the plug's full buoyancy. The diagram explains the working principle of most of the popular types, which can be made in various sizes and of differing shapes.

Fig. 48   Two of the many types of home-made plugs for the handyman

89

The metal lip, or diving vane, is an important factor and must be made of very light material or the plug will become nose heavy. Avoid the use of tin, which will become rusty quickly, and cut it out from thin brass sheeting or aluminium. The two patterns shown are in common usage, but can be altered to suit your own particular ideas.

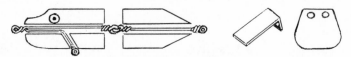

Fig. 49   Plug drilled for wiring

The drillings for the wiring should be as small as possible, on the lines of those shown above. Secure a treble hook to each end of your wire and plan how you are going to set about it before starting.

Effective choices for colouring are a dark greenish blue with a cream belly, or simply brown and gold, and do not worry if your effort falls short of those seen in the shops. You may even like to experiment with various bars and spots imitating eyes and scales, and the fish will not be critical of your artistic efforts providing the action of the plug is lively and attractive.

Worms and Crabs: Artificial resemblances to these are not in any great demand, but they are available from most dealers; they vary considerably in obtaining results, but good captures have been made with them.

Lures resembling (a): Simulations of the sand-eel are often used, made of coloured strips of plastic or other similar material, in various bright colours, and though doubtful baits, they have been known to take fish.

Feathered Lures: Intended to simulate whitebait, brit, and other small fry, these lures have become increasingly popular in recent years. The basis is simply a bunch of feathers wrapped around and tied on to cover a long-shanked hook. Used singly, attached to a short nylon snood, it will be found that a small tinfoil wrapping or lead wire bound round the hook near the eye will help to sink it, and also give it an inviting flash.

A customary mounting is to have from three to six secured on a long trace, in a paternoster style, which is buckled to the reel line.

Fig. 50   Feather lures and a method of mounting them

Construction is simple; tie a pair of feathers, one dark and one light, to each side of an ordinary long-shanked hook (the dark feather being uppermost) to represent a dark back and a light belly, keeping the feathers apart so they do not appear bedraggled. The neck feathers of a cockerel are ideal, but those from a seagull or other bird may be used; If you wish, they may be dyed to any colour, and combinations of red and blue, or blackish blue and white have both proved successful. They are effective in various sizes, up to about 4in, when a treble could usefully be added, and when completed they should be roughly trimmed off to the shape of a fish.

They can provide great sport if used with light tackle with a spiral lead just above them to assist in casting, and in a spinning session, they should be slowly retrieved in alternative methods of sink and draw, so that they flutter about. They can also be trolled with success, but do remember that the weight should be above and not at the end.

Do not hurry in reeling in, for many fish leave deep water to follow them up to mid-water, and then take the bait without mistake; this can also operate in reverse, when they follow them down before taking. They are likely to be less successful in rough water, or from off the beach when the weather is rough.

Spinners: This group of the artificials can be very effective and, again, the 'do-it-yourself' enthusiast can easily and cheaply knock up various patterns from odd scraps of light metal.

These lures, which need no bait, consist of a spinning vane which will rotate around a length of stout wire to which a bead and a treble are attached. They produce a continuous flashing attraction when drawn through the water and may be used at any depth.

A popular and simple type is the elongated shape, made up as shown here, and usually referred to as a 'mackerel spinner'.

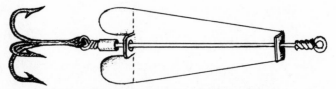

Fig. 51   A popular type of mackerel spinner

It is made up from a single (or sometimes doubled-over) piece of sheet metal—stainless steel or chromed brass is to be preferred—shaped to widen at one end. When cut and filed to size, two cuts are made at the wide end, near the centre, and the resultant middle piece, together with the top end, are both bent back the same side, at right angles, after being pierced to take the wire. When this has been smoothed off, thread the wire and bead it, then secure a treble hook, making sure it is not too small or it will be a poor 'hooker'. The two remaining lugs are then bent over in opposite directions to make the fins. If using a double thickness of metal, a groove is made down the centre of each before soldering together, as the wire will pass through the centre without need to right-angle the ends to take it.

A successful variation of the spinner is the 'wobbler' type which as its name implies, does not revolve, but has a wobbling action to produce a similar attraction. Many anglers consider a good slender wobbler as more effective than the ordinary type spinner, so it could be worthwhile buying or making a couple and trying them out.

Using a 3 by ¾in (approximately) bright metal strip, make two holes about ⅛in in diameter, fit two split rings and a treble hook; curve off one end and smooth off, and bend very slightly at each end as shown (Fig. 52). This will provide the wobble, as at (A). There are various kinds of wobblers which have been given special names, and even the pattern has been modified, as (B), with some variation in the curve, less length, and a hook substituted for the treble.

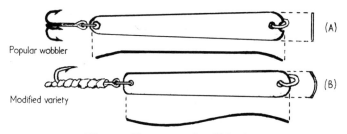

Fig. 52   Two types of wobbler lures

All home made wobblers should be well polished to produce the best results, and if made of any metal that will rust, should be dried off after use. Many anglers believe a lure should spin to be effective, but whilst this may be true of the lighter ones, it is not essential and any heavier or weighted ones that wobble can be just as good as those that spin.

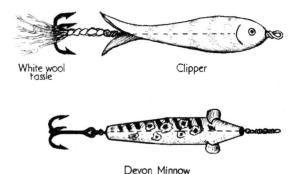

Fig. 53   Two types of ant ferial minnows

Two designs often favoured are the 'Clipper' and the 'Devon Minnow', both facsimiles of fish which have proved very effective. The popular minnow is particularly good for casting, being all metal, and the whole body is bored sufficiently for the nose swivel to slide through it. The idea behind this is that the bored body will move up loosely when a fish is hooked and thus prevent any leverage being used on it to disgorge the hook.

Spoons: There are two main types of spoon baits, the plain spoon which rotates through the water by reason of its own curvature, and the bar spoon which rotates round a wire, either because of its curved shape or by means of spinning vanes.

The plain, or Norwich spoon, is simply a spoon pierced at both ends to take a split ring with a swivel attached at the narrow end, and a split ring with a treble at the wide end. The hook should not be too small, so as to be shielded by the spoon, or it may become a poor hooker.

The fly-spoon is about ¾in long, and holed at the narrow end to take a split ring; a long-shanked hook and a swivel are added to the ring. The spoon should be bright and must have free movement. Some anglers prefer a slightly larger one, 1in long, with a treble and two swivels to connect the split ring.

The flounder spoon is a slight variation of the above but larger in size (in either metal or celluloid), with a single small hook attached to a nylon snood about 6in in length, both being not too far apart.

The bar-spoon, or free spoon, is of the type where the spoon itself swings freely, thus reducing the effect of the spoon shielding the hook. As it swings in an arc it simulates the flash of a larger fish than that of a plain spoon of similar size. The spoon itself revolves round a length of rigid wire, which is loaded with a bead and a small barrel lead, and the end secured to a treble hook. It may be attached direct, or linked on, but the fit must be a loose one.

Fig. 54   Methods of securing spoons

The kidney spoon is a variant of the popular bar spoons, the only difference being in the shape from which it takes its name.

If making up these spoons at home, and for any reason you wish to discard the use of the barrel weight, it will be necessary

VARIOUS TYPES OF SPOONS

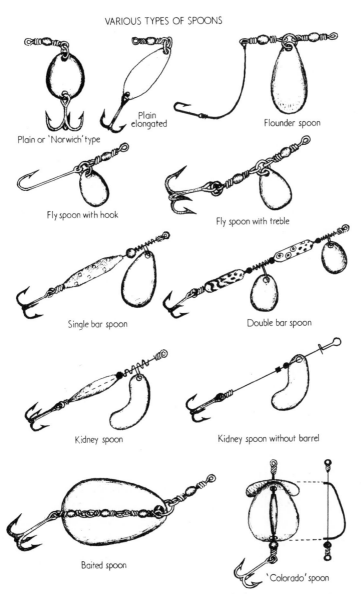

Plain or 'Norwich' type

Plain
elongated

Flounder spoon

Fly spoon with hook

Fly spoon with treble

Single bar spoon

Double bar spoon

Kidney spoon

Kidney spoon without barrel

Baited spoon

'Colorado' spoon

Fig. 55

95

to solder on a stopper as a bead retainer to prevent the spoon descending near the hook.

The Colorado spoon, a very old favourite, is a fast-spinning lure and very effective. It is provided with two projecting ears, or vanes, which are bent slightly in opposite directions to produce the necessary spin. A deepened spoon pierced at each end is used.

The baited-spoon is designed to ensure that the baited hook will not revolve by fitting a series of small swivels in place of the rigid bar. The spoon is thus able to move and turn freely without hindrance and is a superb attraction. A 3in plated spoon has been found to produce the most favourable results, especially when the hook is so positioned that it is just clear of the spoon.

Reverting to the subject of colourings; white is best when daylight is poor, up to dusk; on a brilliant sunny day, use nothing too flashy, but keep to red; if there are no bites about, then try a bait similar to the spoon, eg, herring to silver. Blue has not been found to be very successful, but there is scope here for trial and error.

Give preference to white spoons for bass, and plated ones for flounders. Using spoons from a moored boat, attach a 3-way swivel or fit a spiral lead, get it revolving slowly at the top, then lower it gently by thumbing it off to reach bottom, and then come just up off it. In fast tides use a long span for the lead, but in slack tides shorten this span to position the weight nearer the spoon. Plaice will take the baited spoon from a moored boat, as above or as a drift line, but not when trolled.

A Norwich size 1in, drifted from a moored boat, will often take bass, and a ½in plated or white fly-spoon with an extra swivel added after the split ring to take a size 6 hook will also serve as a baited spoon for these fish. The secret of success with the baited spoon is to troll as slowly as possible, but when anchored, a 3in one about 3ft off bottom is good for bass, and raising it a foot or so may mean encountering dabs. A baited spoon can also be cast from the beach for mullet and bass, but the retrieve must be fairly fast or the mullet will shy away.

Note that a mackerel spinner may also be converted by sub-
stituting a 6 hook in lieu of the treble, and this should be baited
up with a whole 5 or 6in ragworm for bass.

Other useful pointers are:

No flounders may be expected to bite on kidney spoons or any
type that revolves quickly.

Bites on bar spoons are very meagre in harbours.

Bottom or float fishing for flounders is not usually so good in
the summer as it is when they 'go down' in the autumn.

Fish are nearer the bottom at spring tides, and range higher
at neaps.

Jiggers: These are short strip pieces of any flashing metal,
usually about 3 by $\frac{1}{2}$in, drilled in two opposite corners to take
split rings, so causing them to fish erratically. There are two
general types in use, both much alike, but bent differently, and
in one the hook is replaced by a treble.

Fig. 56   Two types of jiggers

Jiggers are very useful for deep trolling, or when using the
'sink and draw' method from an anchored boat in deep water.
A fast tide can make them particularly effective and, if
necessary, the position and amount of bend can be altered.

Finally, if you carry many non-spinning lures loose without
fitted traces, use the sliding loop to join them to your reel line.

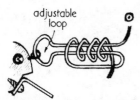

adjustable
loop

Fig. 57   Sliding loop for plug knot

It will not slide under normal pressure but the noose will
close if the strain is excessive; re-open it when brought in.
Form the knot where required and ensure that it is really tight.

97

CHAPTER 8

HINTS AND TIPS FOR ANGLERS

The following is a varied collection of miscellaneous information which may be helpful to the angler on many a fishing expedition.

HANDLE WITH CARE

Weevers: The first dorsal and gill covers are poisonous.

Sting Ray: The whiplike tail and venomous spine can cause temporary paralysis.

Thornback Ray: The barbed tail with curved thorns, and hooked spines on the wings, can wound severely.

Spur Dog: The sharp spur near each dorsal fin can inflict painful gashes.

Bass, Gurnard, Black Bream: The dorsals of these fish are surprisingly sharp and it is advisable always to use a cloth when handling them.

Nearly all wounds caused by fish are liable to turn septic, and remember that both weevers and sting rays remain poisonous even after death.

THE PARTS OF A FISH

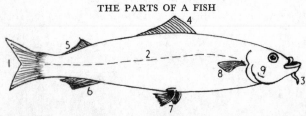

(1) Tail, or caudal fin	(2) Lateral line	(3) Barbel
(4) Dorsal fin (1st)	(5) Adipose fin (2nd dorsal)	(6) Anal fin
(7) Pelvic fin	(8) Pectoral fin	(9) Gill cover

MINIMUM SIZES OF SALT-WATER FISH

The National Federation of Sea Anglers has issued the following schedule of minimum sizes to be observed by members of its affiliated clubs. Fish below these sizes must be returned to the sea by members entering any festival or competition held under its rules and any undersized fish taken to the scales could render the competitor liable to disqualification. These standards could advantageously be accepted by all anglers in the interests of conservation of stocks.

		Boats	Pier or Shore		Boats	Pier or Shore
Bass	... ...	15in	15in	Pollack ...	12in	10in
Bream	... ...	9in	9in	Pouting ...	10in	8in
Brill	... ...	14in	14in	Silver (eel) ...	12in	12in
Bull Huss	...	23in	23in	Spur Dog ...	23in	23in
Coalfish ...	...	12in	12in	Shark (blue)	40lb	40lb
Cod	... ...	12in	12in	Sharks (others)	100lb	100lb
Conger ...	...	28in	28in	Skate ...	5lb	5lb
Dab	... ...	8in	8in	Ray (Thorn-		
Lesser Spotted				back) ...	5lb	5lb
Dogfish	...	18in	15in	Ray (Blonde)	5lb	5lb
Flounder	...	9in	8in*	Smoothound	20in	20in
Garfish ...	...	15in	15in	Sole	9½in	9½in
Gurnard	...	9in	9in	Sole, Lemon	10in	10in
Haddock	...	15in	15in	Scad ...	10in	10in
Hake	... ...	12in	12in	Shad ...	10in	10in
Halibut ...	...	20lb	5lb	Tope ...	20lb	20lb
John Dory	...	13in	13in	Turbot ...	16in	16in
Ling	... ...	28in	28in	Weever ...	8in	8in
Mackerel	...	11in	11in	Whiting ...	10in	10in
Megrim ...	...	10in	10in	Witch ...	11½in	11½in
Monkfish	...	15lb	15lb	Wrasse ...	9in	9in
Mullet ...	...	13in	13in	Unclassified	9in	9in
Plaice ...	...	10in	10in	All other Rays	3lb	3lb

* This may be 10in where so directed by Local Fishery Board.

FISHING DEFINITIONS USED BY ANGLERS

Ballast: A humorous reference to the amount of weight on one's tackle.

Bearing: A directional line from observer to any object.

Boulter, or *Spiller:* A 'long line' set with a series of baited hooks.

Brit: The very immature sprats and pilchards on which many fish prey.

Broke: Said of an angler when his tackle is parted from his reel line.

Courge: The wicker basket or box used to retain live baits in captivity.

Disgorger: A special instrument to facilitate removal of swallowed hooks.

Foul ground: An area where anchor or tackle may easily become snagged.

Foul Hooked: A fish when not hooked by mouth, but elsewhere on its body.

Grammar school fish: The 'educated ones' untempted by your offerings.

Leader: A short nylon length inserted between reel line and tackle to take rough wear and chafing, thus avoiding loss of reel line strength and length.

Killick: A large stone or rock when used in lieu of an anchor.

Marks: Good fishing spots, often located by bearings of permanent landmarks.

Priest: A cudgel or heavy instrument used to stun a fish when brought in.

Scowing: Securing a dinghy anchor at the crown, to trip it when fouled.

Set: A warp tending to put a permanent bend in a wooden rod.

Slub: Drifting seaweed in clumps and masses.

Stop: Any object such as shot, beads, etc affixed on a line to prevent passage.

Streaming: To place and retain a tethered object in the water against tide, etc.

Tailer: A rope or wire loop used to grip round the tail when boating a large fish.

Trot: A planned extended series of baited hooks, pots, boat moorings, etc.

Tubercule: A grisly or bony growth that forms on the skin of some species.

Vraic, or *Wrack:* Various forms of seaweed, such as bladder-rack etc.

Whitebait: The young progeny of the whiting.

White horses: Waves whose tops are turned into breaking crests.

ANGLING LORE

Put a white button on the trace; it will stir up the mud.

Silver paper wrapped around the hook shank will attract fish.

Watch that flock of gulls—where they swoop there are usually fish.

On a pier, follow the tide in; the fish will be moving with it,

The only anglers to catch fish are those whose bait is in the water.

Red wool hanging down over the hook will attract many species of fish.

When the wind is in the east, the fish bite least.

When the wind is off shore, the fishing will be poor.

Where there is one skate, there were always two.

Start your flounder fishing by raking up the mud first.

Ensure your hook never spins with the spoon.

Big fools lay their rods down anywhere for bigger fools to tread on.

When spinning low, always spin slow.

Continuous hail and rain will usually keep fish in deep water.

Fish do not recognise a hook for what it is, so do not be concerned if it is visible.

A shoal of sand-eels in a hurry for the beach is a sure indication that mackerel or pollack are in pursuit.

Do not be deceived by lots of fish splashing about together; it might suggest good sport, but in this mood they are unlikely to want your bait.

Look for any spots where fresh water trickles into the sea; however small it may be, many fish frequent such spots regularly.

Coloured beads set above the hook can be effective when shore fishing, but not from boats.

Bag and hang your rods, never lean them against a wall as they will be liable to warp.

Never lay your rod and reel down on sandy beaches.

HOW TO IDENTIFY FLATFISH

These fish begin life swimming normally as other fish do, but a few weeks after birth the body gradually turns over from the vertical to tilt towards the horizontal, and one eye moves round to meet the other. Until this metamorphosis is complete, they sink to the sea bed to flop around until adjusted to swim in a horizontal plane.

The colour of the upper sides of most is susceptible to change as a form of camouflage, enabling them to blend with their surroundings, and so cannot always be relied upon as a means of identification.

To make certain identification of any one of the following edible fishes, suspend it by its dorsal with coloured surface facing you, and compare these details.

Turbot: The body is very broad and roughly diamond-shaped. The top is brownish coloured, with dark spots, not patterned. It has no scales, but hard tubercules here and there. Eyes on left.

Brill: The body is well rounded, much more so than in the turbot. The top is brown to grey with blotchy spots here and there. Both sides have small smooth scales but no tubercules. Eyes are on the left.

Plaice: Brown on top with well defined red or orange spots haphazard. It has one hard knobly protuberance just behind the eyes. The lateral line is straight; the eyes are on the right.

Flounder: Brown to blackish back, but only some have any orange spots. Some rough thorny tubercules along the base of marginal fins and along the lateral, which is curved at the shoulder, and the whole is covered with a mucus. The underside is an opaque pearly-white surface, smooth all over. The eyes are on the right.

Dab: Sandy brown on top, and some have orange spots. White underneath. Top surface feels like sandpaper. Lateral curves sharply up. Eyes are on the right.

Soles: Many varieties all of long narrow shape with mouth at the end of the snout; the upper jaw projects over the lower one.

IS IT A RECORD?

Many sea fish of record size are denied official recognition because the British Record Fish Committee were not supplied with positive proof of identification, either by clear photographs or production of the fish itself.

As identification is a key factor, a professional photographer, or a really good amateur, is the ideal person to call on, since ordinary snapshots seldom bring out sufficient detail to assist the arbiters. Remember, too, that it is only the fish they are interested in, not the captor proudly displaying it.

Photos should be taken from above the fish, which should be laid out flat on a distinctly contrasting surface. Flat fish should be displayed with the eyed side uppermost; cod, coalfish, and pollack to show a side view of the head displaying chin, barbels, and fins; dogfish need an under-head view also, showing clearly the flaps and teeth, these features being pinned out as necessary so that all are easily discernible. A clearly marked ruler, or rulers, should be laid alongside the fish.

Anyone catching what appears to be a possible record specimen would be well advised to retain it until clear photos have been taken, or the fish identified and measured by a competent biologist, or someone whose qualifications are likely to be equally recognised by the British Record Fish Committee.

Printed lists of existing records are available and claims must be made on the appropriate form obtainable from the Committee. Your tackle dealer will no doubt be pleased to help you in such an event, and if you are a member of a sea-angling club, the secretary certainly will.

'GROUND BAITING' A FISHING PITCH

An often rewarding 'ploy' when fishing a handy beach is to go and select a suitable fishing spot, and note what will be your high-tide fishing position for casting. Then dig a hole some 25 or 30yd off and about 1ft deep, taking a rough bearing between the fishing position and the hole so that you know the direction in which to cast when the tide covers the hole.

Fill the cavity with a mixture of fish offal, crushed crabs, and any other old food scraps well spread out, and bury this by loosely covering it with sand. As the tide rises, it should gradually scour off this covering to release globules of oil to make an attractive trail for fish to pick up and follow.

To ensure you find your mark later on, assemble a rod and line plus one weight; drop the weight in the hole, walk back to your casting spot, and there mark your reel line with wool or sellotape before reeling up again. When you later cast out on the bearing previously taken, drop your tackle just beyond where you think the hole is, reel in until the mark on the line arrives into position, and you should have your bait 'on target'.

A somewhat similar idea can be tried out when rock-fishing, using the old but still effective custom of 'globing'. For this, you first collect a few small jam jars and fill them with a mix of herring or mackerel offal, or any other old surplus bait. The jars are then firmly wedged or jammed between rocks and in crevices at low water, or at water level on a rising tide, near your fishing position. The incoming tide will swirl around the rocks, releasing oil from the jars.

Another useful tip if you know of a likely spot in a tideway that is just out of casting range is to procure a small cylindrical metal screw-top container and bore a hole centrally in top and bottom through which to thread a length of copper or other wire. Twist an eye in one end for the trace, and then solder or secure a weight at the position shown, to keep the trace end cocked, or you could use a pierced bullet outside the tube. Leaving sufficient length to be able to unscrew the cap, pass the wire out through the bottom and make another twisted eye for the reel line. Now screw the cap on, bait up, and with no weight attached permit it to float off as far as wanted. It will slowly fill and sink the bait down when filled; the distance being governed by the size of the holes which can be varied for a slow or quick sink as required. To recast, remove the cap, drain out, and rebait.

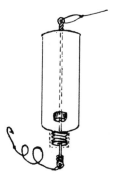

Fig. 59   How to make a 'floataway'

A couple of extra items to weighten your bag could also include some very small corks, cut vertically halfway through to slip on a trace when crabs abound, and also a couple of home-made lures which can be knocked up at home ready for use on baitless days.

The accompanying diagrams, Figs. 60 and 61, which are self explanatory, show: (A) The 'Sole-skin single fly'; (B) The 'Sole-skin sand-eel'; and overleaf (C) The 'Bacon skin cuttlefish'.

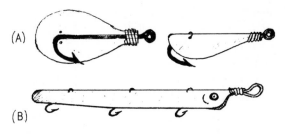

Fig. 60   Home-made lures for baitless days

Fig. 61　The 'Bacon skin cuttlefish'

For (A) and (B) take a strip of flounder or sole, scrape and dry, paint the inside silver, varnish all over, fold down the centre, and whip on.

For (C), soak and scrape thin, using a long hook and thread binding.

SAFETY NOTES FOR DINGHY FISHING

Ensure that your craft is seaworthy, and has positive buoyancy when loaded.

Make a study of the 'Rule of the Road' regulations, and 'Safety at Sea'.

Wear or carry lifejackets, one for each occupant, on all occasions.

Learn the drill for resuscitation, and carry a small first-aid box.

An inboard engine calls for a fire extinguisher, clipped near the tiller.

An outboard engine should be topped up with fuel before departure; do not wait until rolling about later on. Fit a safety lanyard to it, just in case it should become detached and lost overboard.

Always carry oars and crutches, fitted with lanyards made fast inboard.

Master the art of sculling, in case one oar breaks or is lost.

Learn to refrain from standing in small boats, always sit down habitually. If you stand to weigh an obstinate anchor, or boat a hefty fish, any sudden release under your full heaving power could send you sprawling backwards, perhaps overboard.

Never leave without an anchor, learn how to 'scow' it, and see that your rope for it is three times the greatest depth you may cover, to avoid dragging. If possible, fit a roller on the stem of the dinghy and make sure the rope is secured at both ends before casting out the anchor or weight.

Provide a large, flat bait-box and receptacles for all fish taken so that your boat is kept clean inboard and not slimy with messy bait.

Fit a false skeg to your rudder to give warning that you are about to ground in shallows or over hard bottoms. They are nailed on loosely, detach on impact, and may be recovered.

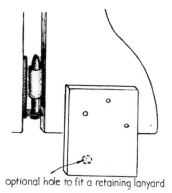

optional hole to fit a retaining lanyard

Fig. 62   False skeg on rudder

CHAPTER 9

SELECTIVE FISHING

Once having mastered the general techniques of sea angling from pier, beach, rocks or dinghy, there are many anglers who may decide to specialise in a certain species of fish and prefer to become an adept at taking these to the exclusion of all others.

There are at least half-a-dozen or so species that attract such selective search, and the following brief descriptions of their habits and of some of the more popular methods of capturing them may be helpful to those who decide to take up this form of specialisation.

FISHING FOR BASS

Bass first appear in late April, near the surface, then gradually go down to roam around until early autumn, when they range further inshore to spawn. Thus August and September are particularly good months for taking them.

If possible, the angler should study a chart of his locality, noting gullies, sandy expanses and, especially, areas of broken ground and rocks in harbours and adjoining shores where established growths of seaweed are frequently searched by bass in quest of the small fish which congregate there to feed. He should also try to ascertain which are the best marks for there will certainly be many special spots in the locality known to the 'regulars', such as wrecks, pipes, sunken piles, outfalls, fast water races, eddies, and fresh water outlets, where bass are known to congregate.

The most favourable weather conditions are a dull day with slight wind just ruffling the surface, for sunlight glaring strongly through a flat, calm surface reduces your prospects. An on-shore wind usually brings the bass closer inshore (spring tides being best), whilst the better times to fish are early morning, late evening, and during the night. The clearer the water the deeper the fish are, whilst gales will drive them out to deeper water away from the beaches. After a stormy blow has sub-sided they will venture much further inshore, and long casting will not be necessary as they will be milling around in the back-wash scour of the surf as it exposes the marine life they seek.

The bass is a lively hunter, and generally travels alone once it becomes mature, always searching for food. They seek their sustenance both on the bottom and at mid-water, seldom re-maining in one place, but will rise to the surface whenever shoals of brit or sand-eels are about.

The choice of rod is not easy to advise, and every experienced angler will have his own distinct preference. For school bass, a light rod will give you good sport, but if there is a possibility of large fish in the offing, a more sturdy outfit will be needed. Bass have large mouths, so use large hooks.

The living sand-eel on a drift line is undoubtedly the best method; use an 8 or 10lb trace, 7 or 8ft long, with a No 1 hook attached, and just sufficient weight, ½oz or so, to keep the bait under the surface. Pay out your line slowly to stream well astern and be prepared to tighten up at any moment for the take will be with a sudden rush when you employ this method. Immediately you have struck and can feel he is hooked, let him make his initial run before you start to get him under control.

If legering, do not anchor your bait to the sea bed, but so arrange your tackle that it swirls about freely, as a bass bait should be a moving one. When float fishing, live bait, such as prawns or sand-eels, are certainly best and the rod should be kept in hand with no slack line drooping. If over rocky terrain, keep the rod well up and the line taut, for here he will adopt a different strategy and head for the rocks to smash you up. Spinning is another popular technique, especially in calm con-ditions; various lures may be tried out, but if the weather worsens then windswept line, loss of bait, and clumps of sea-weed may nullify your efforts.

Beach fishing for bass is one of the great attractions of the sport, but do not, as a matter of course, always cast out 'behind the breakers', assuming the bass will be there, without first considering that on a deep sloping shore the food they seek is carried well out by the undercurrent, so that a long cast will be needed. But on a flat shore, where the scouring is not so strong, the food is not carried so far, and so your cast could be shortened. If it is rough, it will be best to keep to one hook on a short trace, so that it runs freely and there is no risk of tangling up multiple hooks.

A popular end tackle for beachcasters is a 3 to 4ft trace fitted with two hooks, size 1/0 and 2/0, used with a pear-shaped bomb weight to roll around and cover an area. If the tide is strong, use a pipe or barrel lead, and always have a net handy for even if he is not properly hooked you may still be able to land him if you act quickly.

The best baits are those they like and which are common to your locality; these may include sand-eels, squid, slipper limpet, prawns, and small 1in green crabs, whilst jumper rag, lasks, softbacks, razor fish and mussels are all taken. To this host of good offerings could be added bloaters and kippers, and many other fish baits, whilst many oddities such as fat bacon, sausage, even cucumber and banana, have all had success. Baits need not be fresh, as they will be taken even if 'high', but the fresher they are the better, both for you to handle and for bass to fancy.

Fig. 63   Fly-spoon tackle for bass

The above useful stand-by bass outfit could easily be assembled at home and consists of a fly-spoon ¾in long, two swivels, three split rings, and a size 5 or 6 hook attached to a trace 2ft or so in length. You may like to adorn the hook with a few woollen strands, either white, or red and yellow, wrapped on with fuse wire, and for casting, add a foldover anti-kink weight. It can be equally effective when used from pier, jetty, dinghy, or beach.

FISHING FOR BREAM

Bream may be found at all depths between bottom and mid-water. They are unlikely to be interested in any clumsily arranged tackle or bedraggled-looking baits, and as they have comparatively small mouths, light gear presenting small entice-ments is called for.

Popular methods range from drifting or tripping a lead with just sufficient weight to overcome the tide, to driftlining a single hook or paternoster, (not the brass boom type). Attach a swivel below the lead to take a 5 or 6ft trace and use a single long-shanked size 6 or 8 hook, which is easier to unhook and enables you to get down again quickly.

A sliding pater hook could also be used to vary the fishing depth, lifting it up off the bottom when the lead bumps and changing its position as necessary. Many adopt the practice of rigging the trace up, streaming it away on the tide, and then adding weight and gradually lowering it by rod manipulation to search at differing depths. Others prefer to begin by concen-trating on the bottom first, reeling up a foot at a time. Here one counts the turns in case of success, so that if bites are coming one can repeat and come off-bottom to the same depth. In many methods the 3-way swivel is often used with a flowing trace, but should the tide slacken this could foul up, so have a boom handy.

The best baits are worms, mussels, squid, sand-eel, or oily fish strips about $1\frac{1}{2}$ by $\frac{1}{2}$in, very thin and hooked only once, through the end. Bites, usually called 'knocks', vary from a strong jerk and quick pull, to a series of vigorous quick jerks as the fish shakes its mouth.

Dinghy anglers, when in a tideway, could use a 'rubby-dubby' bag, either lowered over the side or secured above the anchor, and when fishing over rocks it is a good idea to have a small sack of stones lightly bound and tied to the anchor rope. It can easily be broken if snagged, and could save both your anchor and your temper.

FISHING FOR COD

The cod is a ground feeder, usually caught on the bottom hook, but is sometimes taken in mid-water. Few large ones are taken in a depth of less than ten fathoms, but the younger codling come quite close inshore to feed and may be taken from beaches, seawalls, and piers, though boat fishing is usually more profitable.

The best times are after sunset on very dull days, and best results come from beaches when the sea is a bit choppy. Do not cast too far out, and search behind those breakers amidst the backscour.

A strong rod is essential, and whether using a pater or leger, do use stout gear and fit large hooks, combined with a good weight to keep your tackle down. Cod continually root about in the sea bed for their food and a strong, single, well-baited hook well down on the bottom is most likely to bring success.

They live mainly on squid, herring, mackerel, and sand-eels, but will also take worms, crustaceas, and molluscs; slipper limpets, sprats and crab are favoured in some localities, and a live pouting on a paternoster can be very attractive to them, but all baits should be fresh. Mussels, where plentiful, can also be successful.

A big mouthful could mean a big fish, or a cocktail of two different baits might fetch them, but if using only worms, then a bunch of half-a-dozen together on the hook may be required to interest a big fish.

When you feel a bite, strike hard when the fish starts to draw off line. If you strike too soon you will jerk the bait from its mouth because it draws its food in by gulping it down with its mouth partially open. Hold your rod all the time to make sure of hooking codling, for they will very often just snatch and run. Keep a tight line on and beware of their ability to regurgitate both bait and hook by shaking their heads as they reach the surface.

FISHING FOR CONGER

Most anglers prefer to seek this fish by legering a running trace, or using a boom to permit it to take line when examining the bait without moving the lead. Large hooks are essential, one often being preferred to two, and use a large bait 5 to 6ft below the lead, (expendable type), all well swivelled on a nylon-covered steel trace to withstand teeth and rock wear.

Over rocky terrain, try 3 to 5ft off bottom, now and again swimming the bait, especially if it is a live one such as a pouting hooked through the tail or dorsal. All bait should be fresh, for conger are apt to be fastidious; fresh squid or cuttle (beaten to soften it), or any fish bait is good, but whatever you use, be generous.

Remember that a good conger, when played, not only fights and pulls but will deliberately twist and spin, quite often wrapping itself up in your tackle.

In his approach, he is usually very cautious and will nudge the bait, mouth it a little, or expel it in his uncertainty, so note any slight movements of your rod-tip that may indicate this, pay out a little slack and be alert for that steady pull as he moves away with it. Then strike well home to penetrate and hold firm. If he is on, you will have no doubt about it as the action commences.

Congers will seize any opportunity to dash for a refuge at the least sign of any let-up on your part, so get it off bottom as soon as you can, to prevent it lashing its tail around the rocks as an anchor hold.

When boating your fish, gaff him just behind the head if you are unable to lift him in easily by rod, and if it is a really heavy one and your boat is small, bring it in over the stern. He may be difficult to control, so try to stun him with a priest, hitting on the tail vent to create an opportunity to stick a sharp knife into his brains. Then lower him into an open sack and if you are apprehensive, or until you become an expert, dont try taking the hook out, but stow him away trace and all until you come ashore.

FISHING FOR FLOUNDERS

This has become a popular sport in areas containing sandy or mud bottoms, especially in harbours where you can move about at will in a dinghy over a large expanse and explore inlets and gullies. Pater, leger, and float are all successful methods, but gear must be as light as possible to enjoy good sport, wherever you fish from.

Flounders are not choosy about baits and will readily take rag or lug most months, whilst hermit crab is the most deadly at all times. The effectiveness of baits can vary with the seasons, the soft back crab being good in the spring, slipper in the summer and autumn, and any white or yellow bait such as slipper, razor, and even tripe could be added in the colder months.

Flounders do not bite greedily, but gently mouth the bait around a bit before taking it all in. When on the bottom they will often hook themselves without any sign being given of their attempts to disgorge the hook.

For shore fishing, the best times are the early floods, when they enter shallow water to seek their food, so it may not be necessary to cast far beyond this; as the tide rises this area will be enlarged, and as casting distance increases, reel in a yard or two occasionally to stir up the bottom. Over sand and mud this will create a cloud as the weight drags along over the bottom, thus forming an attraction (use a 'grip' type lead, as the torpedo casting type will usually only cut a groove).

When fishing from a pier or jetty it will also pay to 'follow the tide in' and work near the inshore areas rather than the deeper water end; as this is the practice of the moving fish, you should follow suit.

The dinghy angler, armed with a few floats and spoons to augment his bait, has several techniques at his disposal, especially in creeks, many of which can also be used from the shore.

In a dinghy, a spot of trolling before anchoring could well be rewarding. The boat is rowed or paddled very slowly, with the tide, so that the spoon does not revolve more than three turns per yard of progress; should the spoon turn too fast then very few fish will show any interest.

The 'trolled baited spoon' is considered one of the best of all methods; use a 6ft trace with a light weight and swivel at the reel line and an attachment loop for the spoon at the other. Try midwater to bottom.

When fed up with paddling, the boat may be permitted to drift with the tide, and now the baited spoon could be used with or without a float, or used as a light leger, and kept just off the bottom so that it covers as much ground as possible. Flounders often wait at gully ends for tide to turn.

Once anchored, there are several techniques one may employ, a popular one being the floating spoon method. For this, use a free-running float and a 5ft trace with a single hook attached to the reel line by a swivel; A 2 or 3in plated spoon is then mounted about 3in from the hook (this distance should not be increased or it will greatly lessen the effect). When made up separately to a split ring, and then held by the trace, this is known as a 'flounder spoon'.

Either the baited spoon or flounder spoon may be used, and best results are obtained with about 3in of worm hanging from the hook. It is the wobbling of the spoon in the tideway that moves the bait and induces a take.

Another method is the floating pater, consisting of two booms rigged pater style, on which the weight will be used to scrape along the mud and stir up an occasional cloud. The lower hook is arranged to swim 6 to 9in above it, and a flounder spoon on the hook above.

A wandering float tackle consists of either a single trace, pater, or a spoon, swivelled to the reel line and suspended from a float as a perpendicular plummeted line; it may be given scope to wander away some distance.

A flounder can move very fast after a spoon, and will given an unmistakeable signal to you on float tackle if you are on the look-out for it. As it mouths the bait your float will wobble and tremble for several seconds as it takes the bait in, after which the float will take a rapid dive; strike now and it should be yours.

Flounders will take a baited spoon supported by a float, but are chary and shy when a spoon is allowed to drift on its own without a float. There are also several types of 'wander-tackle' to choose from. Two of these are described below, but there are many others you can make up with a little skill and ingenuity.

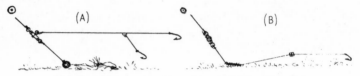

Fig. 64   Two types of 'wander tackle' for flounders

(A) is simply a two-hook trace and a light bouncing weight that will enable it to get around easily over a large area. (B) is a single-hook trace with a light spiral, sufficient to keep it down yet not become buried in mud and unable to be moved around by the tide. Any type you use to cast well out should incorporate a pronged torpedo-type lead to scratch up those clouds, and will prove ideal in shallow waters.

One of the greatest failings of many beginners is too much haste in getting the fish in. As soon as any movement is felt they make a great swoop of the rod and start reeling in—a fatal error if a flounder is just about to take.

FISHING FOR MACKEREL

The best times are early morning or at dusk, and keep in mind that a moving bait is the most tempting, although not essential.

Several techniques can be employed, the most popular methods being trolling, spinning, and float fishing. Start your quest just under the surface and then go down by 3ft stages. If not there, they could be right on the bottom, for middle waters seldom contain many fish, and the reason for this depth searching is that mackerel will see a bait above, but not below them.

If dinghy fishing, troll slowly with an ordinary 'mackerel spinner' streamed out about 25 yards or so, first trying a 1oz weight and a trace as long as you can manage. A small spoon, sand-eel, or squid tentacle about 6ft down could also be tried as a useful change.

Spinning is another good method, in which you allow the boat to drift as you cast about in different directions to cover a wide area, or anchor the boat and search different depths. If you spot a shoal from your boat, keep outside it and you can't miss when you cast in, whereas if you plough right through them, they will surely scatter.

Driftlining is fine sport, using a 9 hook on a 6ft trace, weighted to keep just below the surface. Float fishing from any good position can also be rewarding; try using a slim float with fish strip or small rag on the hook about 3ft under; hold the rod, do not fish too far away and strike quickly as soon as a bite is felt.

Another good lure is the feathered one (see p. 91), either single or as a trot arranged to flow out or rigged up as a pater. Also effective at times is the common red and gold milk top, moving about just above the hook.

FISHING FOR MULLET

This is a worthwhile sport calling for its own technique and specially prepared tackle. Select your lightest, whippiest rod, about 8ft long, and your lightest suitable reel, so that when rigged up you should register the slightest tremor. Size 9 hooks, 4 to 8lb breaking-strain line, some split shot and a sliding float complete the assembly, and a landing net is also a necessity.

You will require some groundbait to attract these fish, so prepare a mixture of finely chopped stale bread, fish cuttings, crushed crabs, etc, which could be laced with a touch of pilchard or codliver oil. For the hook bait the best is a small 1in ragworm, especially on float tackle, but bread paste, fish liver, peeled shrimps, macaroni, tripe, small crust baptised with fish paste, are all suitable.

For surface fishing, plain bread crust is good, and a stiff

bread paste with pilchard or anchovy flavour can also be effective. If you make up a ball of paste, orange size, and take a few crusts of bread as a change, you should be well equipped for a whole day's fishing.

Two points to bear in mind is never to splash your bait in near them, or to offer a bait that is too big for their small mouths; their stomachs are capable only of dealing with vegetable or soft matter, and therefore any hard bait will be ignored. They like soft baits and mouth it about a bit before making a decision.

Choose a likely spot in which to settle down quietly, and throw in small pieces of bread to interest any that may be in the vicinity. If they are not on the surface and there is no movement below, rig up a light pater with small hooks and probe at varying depths. Do this even if there are no signs of fish around, and at the same time gently cast in, without a plop, a few handfuls of groundbait, for mullet feed at all levels from the surface to the bottom.

If they should rise and feed near the top, then small pieces of cork on your line will keep your bait up near them. You could be prepared for such a situation by rigging up at home some such plan as illustrated below, which can quickly be assembled using biro ink tubes through cut corks or candles.

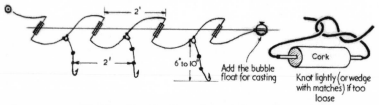

Fig. 65   Details of a cork trace for mullet

Mullet will not usually show interest if the baits are more than 1ft below the surface, but will maintain their inquisitiveness if they are presented to them at their cruising level near the top, where they only have to open their mouths to try it. If possible, place your tackle out ahead of them where it can drift to them with the tide, and keep repeating this drill. When you do get a take, draw the fish quietly away and net it with as little disturbance to the rest of the shoal as possible.

A modified version could be arranged for casting by adding a bubble-float at the end of a trace with small hooks on very short snoods arranged just above it; cast beyond the spot required so that the splash of the impact is not over your anticipated quarry.

A light inconspicuous float, carrying a hook with a split shot stopped just above it and suspended about 9in from the surface, should keep the bait at just the right level for success, but becomes less effective if the water is choppy as bites may not be felt. If the tide starts carrying your baited hook away from the groundbait area, try changing to a pater. A pater with ½in square portions of crust, or a paste ball a little smaller than that, used in a sink and draw manner, will often capture them.

Mullet always approach a bait cautiously, sucking it from the side rather than from underneath, so if you cannot actually see him it is good policy to strike at every tremor. But if he is in sight, let him take the hook well into his mouth before you strike.

A good-sized fish, once hooked, will rush off at once, so remember that you are using very light gear, and do not attempt to stop him as he may be big enough to break you. Yield line until you can obtain control, then draw him towards you and *net* him; do not try to lift him in if this can be avoided as some have a hard lip attached by a soft skin which they extend to suck the bait, and many are lost by the lip being pulled away by a hard jerk. When striking, do not swipe hard; just a firm quick pull for the barb to penetrate, then ease sufficiently to retain the hold and the bend of your rod will help cushion the effect if he runs.

One can also have good sport spinning for mullet, and the best tackle to use is now thought to be the French mullet spoon, rigged as shown in Fig. 66.

If going dinghy fishing for mullet, all noise and movements should be kept to a minimum, even to allowing the boat to drift down to your planned anchorage. Even the use of oars

will drive them away and the anchor should be lowered carefully and quietly. Warm, calm, settled weather is best for mullet
fishing, and they become increasingly difficult to catch as the
cold weather comes along.

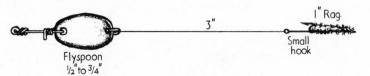

Fig. 66   A French mullet spoon

FISHING FOR PLAICE

Settled conditions and warm weather combine to give the
best chances of success, when results should appear between
three hours before high water and up to two hours after. The
best fish are nearly always to be found on the sand, especially
large, hard, patchy expanses.

Paternoster tackle is the first choice, using long-shanked
hooks which are easier to unhook. But do not have them too
large and suspend them on nylon snoods about 9in long, arrang-
ing the lowest one to be about 1ft from the sea bed. Some may
prefer to use a boom and trace, or arrange a roving trace, but
these will only be effective so long as the tide can stream them
out. With either of these methods, frequently resort to the sink
and draw method on and off bottom, slowly and evenly raising
the rod tip for the movement. In deeper water, use a long, free-
flowing trace, and spoons can often bring results; try a white
spoon over any uneven ground.

The best time for casting is on windless days, when plaice
come a bit further into the shallows, often burying themselves
in the sand with a spectacular sweep of the tail, either completely, or just peeping up.

From groynes and piers a roving tackle tripping over the
bottom when suspended from a float can give good sport, but
do not strike at the first bob of the float, unless it then disappears,
taken by some other species.

Plaice do not like rough weather, or being bombarded with

shingle as they lie in the shallows, and will then retreat to deep water where they are harder to find. When boat fishing, start at low tide and move in with it hourly.

Most of these two species live in deep water, beyond the shore fringe area of the dinghy angler, but as some do occasionally come in close and many are taken by beachcasters, they deserve mention.

Both skates and rays winter in deep water, but in April the first to return are the thornbacks, and the others soon follow, all being on the move in the spring. They will still be keeping deep in the main, but may start venturing closer inshore after dark, and a low tide over a sandy shore offers the best prospect.

The tackle must be strong, so use a fine wire or strong nylon trace with one or two large and well-baited hooks. You have a choice between using a roving trace, a stationary bait, or some method of slow intermittent movement; either or all could be tried but remember always to keep the bait right down.

Large baits are the secret; a whole herring or large fillets, fresh or frozen, is a general choice, though mackerel, wrasse, or bream will do. They will also take hermits, shellfish, and sand-eels, but if using worms then a good bunch is called for to offer an adequate mouthful.

These fish do not bite heavily, but usually drop over the bait with a gentle flop to devour it. Many fish are lost through being over-hasty, so that the fish is foul-hooked in the wing as the bait is dragged along from under it.

Once hooked they can offer great resistance, gliding and flapping in an attempt to reach the bottom and hug it by wing suction. A steady pull should lift it off, followed by a session of steady 'pumping' it up. A gaff should be used to bring it in, and immediately it has been unhooked, get down again as they frequently travel in pairs. If you should hook a large one when alone in a dinghy, remember the previous advice and bring it to the stern rather than risk a capsize in the excitement of **boating it amidships.**

CHAPTER 10

FISH RECOGNITION AND HABITS

Excluding the deeper water fish such as halibut and hake, and the various other species of wanderers which occasionally lose their way and come inshore, there are over thirty species (many of which have more than one variety), that can be taken around the shores of the British Isles. Brief descriptions of them and their habits have here been arranged in alphabetical order for easy reference, together with an illustration to assist identification. The freehand drawings are not proportionate in scale to each other.

Angler-fish. This ugly-looking creature, also known as the fishing frog, or frogfish, may occasionally be taken on rod and line.

It has a large head, broader than it is long, a short tapering body, and a wide mouth with the lower jaw noticeably protruding. Suspended from the head is a filament of skin with a small flap on the end, which it protrudes and twitches to attract small fish to investigate. Whereupon the jaws immediately clamp down on the unsuspecting visitor. It may be found in most British waters and has a habit of using its large pectoral fins to scoop out depressions in mud or sand, where it will remain partially hidden waiting for its prey to approach near enough to be seized. They can thus be found close inshore at times, especially outside tidal estuaries, where they lie in wait for fish moving out with the tide.

Method, tackle and bait will all be whatever you happen to be using at the time, as no one would set out to catch them deliberately. They do not confine themselves to bottom feeding, so may be caught at any depth, though they are not prolific.

They could be described as the least discriminating of our coastal fish in their choice of food, almost every variety of bait having been found in their stomachs, and have been known to have choked themselves by swallowing something too large for even their big mouths to encompass.

Should you ever happen to catch one, do remember that they can remain alive out of water, playing possum for a long time. So take great care, and beware of the dangerous teeth within those powerful jaws, which may suddenly attempt to snap at your hands or feet.

Bass. Although one may be able to distinguish between a blunt-nose type and the sharp-nosed variety, there is only the one true bass; a noble fish which can develop magnificent proportions and possesses unparalleled fighting qualities.

Its colour is dark blue to blackish grey on its back, shading to silvery sides, and an almost white belly. The tail fin is well marked and it has two dorsals, the first being very prickly indeed.

With few exceptions, they are to be found in southern waters and as far north as Anglesey on the west and the Humber to the east. They usually arrive in May on their annual inshore visit for spawning and depart on the approach of winter, although many of the bigger ones remain and have been captured in sandy bays during the cold winter months. They prefer fast-moving water.

The small fish are called school-bass, or shoal-bass, weighing up to about 2lb, but the average good fish is from 5 to 8lb, whilst there are plenty of good specimens about that reach double figures. In the early spring, school-bass will often forage around rocks, their quarry being the crabs which are mating and shedding their shells.

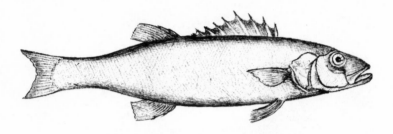

Their young seem to grow quickly, after which they slow down, taking about ten years to reach the 4lb mark. In general the young tend to keep close inshore in shoals during their first year, but they leave as they get older, first congregating in smaller groups of similar-sized fish, and then gradually splitting up, eventually becoming single roamers. Most anglers regard this fish as offering the best sport of all and the methods and techniques of catching them have been described on p. 108.

Bream. There are two varieties of this species which appear regularly around the British Isles; though one or two visitors of other but similar varieties are occasionally caught.

The Common Sea-Bream, sometimes called the Red Bream, has a deep thick body with a high single dorsal fin; the upper parts are reddish, the sides and underparts silvery, and it has a black spot on its gills at the commencement of the lateral line. It has a small mouth, with both frontal and side teeth, and their young, which grow to a length of up to 8in in their first year, are known as chad.

Another variety of the same species is the Black Bream: sometimes called Old Wife. It has a bluish grey back and a silver belly, usually with horizontal golden bands running below the lateral. Both types are covered with scales, and anything over 3lb is a good fish.

Bream live through the winter in deep water, and they begin coming inshore in shoals about the middle of May, all those of similar size tending to keep together and congregate over rocky or weedy grounds. The Red Bream abounds on the south and west coasts.

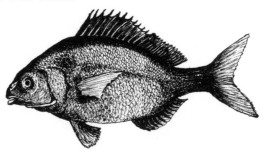

By mid-June the season is in full swing and the black bream's annual visit to its Channel spawning area is a regular and outstanding sporting attraction, though it is a rare visitor north of this area. Bream are usually gone by the end of September, and though the adult fish offer good sport, anglers are glad to see the back of the hordes of young which continually strip baits from all hooks in the vicinity.

Take care when handling these fish as the leading edge of the dorsal is very sharply spined and a small handcloth is advisable.

Brill. One of the larger British flatfishes, the brill is somewhat like a turbot, but slightly more rounded so that it is almost oval in shape.

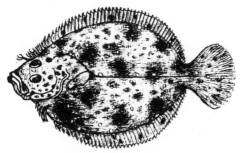

The upper side varies from brown to grey, with blotchy patches here and there, whilst the underside is white; it has smooth scales on both sides, but there are no bony tubercles. The eyes are on the left, and the lateral line on the upper surface curves away from the gills. It has a deep-cut mouth.

Brill are to be found all round the coast, especially in the south, and being a deep-water fish, it favours depths of twenty to forty fathoms over sandy or muddy bottoms. In the summer, however, it will come much further inshore, where it frequents sandy bays and is often to be found foraging on the down-tide side of sandbars.

Methods, tackle, bait are similar to those used when seeking turbot. Legering with a 4ft trace is a popular method, and as brill feed mainly on small fish and the occasional crustacea, these should be the bait offered to them. Sand-eels, fish strips, and worms are all acceptable, but keep your bait as active as possible as they prefer a moving one. Brill become mature when they reach around the 12in mark; a good brill will average around 4lb and the larger ones about 7lb.

Cod. Various names are used to classify cod according to their weight and size. The small specimens of only a few pounds are termed 'codling' until they mature, whilst 'poor cod' are just that, less than 12in, shallow bodied and fork-tailed. 'Scally Cod' is the nickname applied to all those with freak streaks or spots, or of unusual shapes.

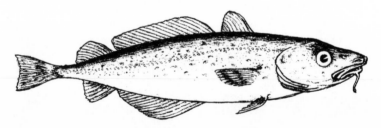

Colour may vary according to the ground where the fish is caught, but in general it is from olive yellow to brown red, and speckled with dark marble spots; it has silvery undersides and the lateral line is white. All cod possess a large mouth, over which the snout projects, and there is a barbel under the lower jaw.

Cod are plentiful around northern British shores, more especially in late autumn and winter, but less abundant on the south coast, where they occasionally appear as winter approches. Of recent years, however, they have been coming south in increasing numbers.

There would appear to be a summer run inshore of fish full of spawn from May onwards, with shoals of small ones appearing in the late summer. A winter run of specimens begins in late October, and by December, when there are many such larger ones about, they become one of the chief attractions of winter fishing.

Cod are bottom feeders on anything eatable, preferring squid and mussels, and will follow close behind shoals of any fish for their food. Large hooks with large baits could mean large cod, but with smaller hooks offer them a cocktail of generous proportions, and in all cases remember not to strike in a hurry. The best fishing is from boats.

Conger. The colouration of a conger changes according to the ground on which it lives, and will vary from all shades of grey to black. The younger fish show a pink tinge which darkens gradually after they attain a length of about 1ft.

The conger has a wide mouth and the top and bottom jaws are set with very sharp teeth; it has no pelvic fins and no scales, but is formidable and ferocious in appearance. Actually it is a timid fish, very easily scared by sudden noises, but do not be deceived by this as, when hooked, it can be both cunning and strong in action and never lets up.

Distribution is plentiful throughout British waters, and although many small fish are taken, there are numerous double-figure specimens about. They will be found haunting deep, rocky grounds, where they lurk amongst the crevices and weeds, and also among old wrecks or other sea bed obstructions. They feed mainly at night, and the darkness of deep waters is where the big ones are most likely to be found. They may also be caught from harbour walls and piers, but these will not be large ones as a rule.

Congers have the ability to remain alive a long time out of the water, and even an apparently dead one can sometimes be dangerous. Its alleged bark is a fallacy, the sound being caused simply by the air bladder wheezing as the eel struggles. Another word of warning for beginners is never to wear light thin shoes or to fish in bare feet, for if a conger should get loose in a small boat you could be in for some nasty bites.

Dab. Sometimes called Garve, there are two distinct varieties of this species. In the Common, or Sand Dab, as illustrated, the lateral line curves upwards, above the pectoral and this is the one most frequently caught by anglers. The other, the Long Rough Dab has a very slightly curved lateral line and some rough brownish spots on its underside near the tail. Some have orange spots which are darker and smaller than those on a plaice.

Both are white underneath, the ridge behind the eye is smooth, and they do not exceed 18in in length. Their small scales become rough to the touch as they mature.

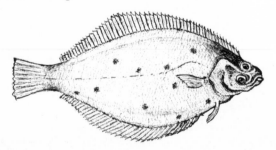

Dabs may be found all round the shores of the British Isles except in rocky areas. They spawn from March to May, and by September there are numerous small ones in many shallow sandy areas. The mature ones move out to deeper water in the spring as the warmer weather begins, to spawn and return later. They will often enter estuaries when winter arrives.

Dabs prefer a sandy bottom, where they feed on shellfish, worms, starfish, mussels, small crabs, etc, as their standard diet. They will also take hermits and razor fish, and sometimes, meat, but not fish baits. They usually swim about 4ft off bottom, but when feeding they go around stirring up the bottom vigorously, so that it will probably pay you to do likewise with a spiral or button on your trace.

The wind will often upset their feeding routine, in which case it will be advisable to come just off bottom and move your tackle around to attract their curiosity. A high tide at dusk is generally considered as the most favourable time.

Dog-fish. There are two common species, one rarer, and two types scientifically classed in other families but included among dogfish by most anglers. Generally referred to as the 'angler's pests', all have a very rough skin, and are found over mud, sand or gravel.

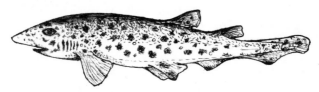

A Nurse Hound, or Greater Spotted Dogfish

The most common of the two species is the Nurse Hound, which is also variously known as the Greater Spotted Dogfish, Bull Huss, or Bounce. It dislikes shallows and prefers broken ground.

The Rough Hound, also called the Lesser Spotted Dogfish, Robin Huss, or Rowhound, prefers sandy bottoms, where it seeks worms and small fish.

Both types arrive with the warmer weather, moving off to deeps in winter, and though they are somewhat similar, idenity can be established by comparing the spots, then turning them over to examine details as shown in Fig. 67 overleaf.

129

The third and rarest type is the Black-Mouthed Dogfish, which is aptly named.

The Spur Dog, or Piked Dog, belonging to a different family, has no anal fin, and is easily distinguishable by a sharp spur preceding each dorsal fin which can inflict a very nasty wound.

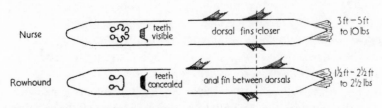

Fig. 67   Identification points between Nurse and Rowhound

So kill it immediately it is boated, and remember that it can curl itself amazingly in an effort to strike out with its spurs; cut off and ditch them if you intend to keep the fish. They come inshore during the summer from deeper water, averaging 2ft and growing up to 4ft, and usually travel in shoals, attacking any fish on or off hooks, and even their own kind.

The Smooth Hound, an upper water inhabitant, is a small shark resembling a tope; it has light spots above the lateral, and grows to 6ft.

Never hold a dogfish by its tail, for some can writhe and bite you.

Eel. Though sometimes called the Yellow Eel, or Silver Eel, there is only one kind, the colours merely indicating different life phases.

The Common Eel is widely distributed in British waters, and may turn up at any time and in any place. Though spending part of its life in fresh water, it is born at sea and always returns there.

On the flood tide, eels tend to keep near the bottom, where they will forage along the edges of gullies, then advance on to the mudbanks as the water starts covering them. When the tide turns and starts the run off, they hasten to leave the shallows and banks and make for mid-channel, where they are swept down in the main course of the tide, very often well up in the water near the surface.

The best method of fishing for them is to use a pater or leger on the flood or at slack water, but fish well up on the run out. Any normal baits may be used, but herring strips generally take preference over worms, with softbacks as an alternative. Eels will often take a baited spoon $1\frac{1}{2}$ to 2in in size, but seem to lose interest if a larger size is used.

The feel of a bite from an eel is different from that of other fish, being one or two fierce tugs, followed by a solid, powerful pull. As you strike, it will writhe about fighting ferociously to get to the bottom and find refuge, and if a large one, will resist every inch of the way up. When it appears near the surface, lift it clear of everything, as it will leap and twist and turn in the air if possible, and should it touch any object affording leverage it could well free itself and escape. Stun it quickly before it can get your gear into a hopeless tangle.

Flounder. The commonest of our flatfish, flounders do not grow to heavyweights, and being fairly plentiful and good to eat are sought by many anglers, some of whom will devote expeditions solely to their capture.

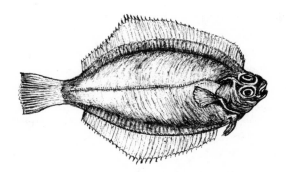

Also called the Fluke, or White Fluke, the flounder will vary in colour from one locality to another, its back ranging from deep brown darkening out to black. Some have orange spots, but these are usually dull, and generally disappear when the fish is taken from the water.

The underside is an opaque pearly white, smooth all over, and there are some rough tubercules along the base of the marginal fins and the lateral line, which is curved at the shoulder. The whole of the back is covered with a mucus and the fish has its eyes on the right.

Flounders may be found in areas adjacent to nearly all shores of the British Isles, and especially in muddy harbours and river estuaries. They hug the bottom, often burying themselves, or laying in wait, looking upwards, and therefore expect to see their food above them. They like moving water and also prefer a moving bait.

They move off to spend cold winters in deeper waters, returning after spawning. They do not all depart at the same time and will be going to and coming back to their local grounds from March to June, being away for about ten to twelve weeks. On their return, they may be found several feet off the bottom, whilst it is known that in the autumn they will 'go down', and tend to keep on the bottom before leaving again. It is worth remembering that they love venturing into fresh water estuaries and inlets, as they can survive in either fresh or salt water.

Garfish. A fish of many names this, variously known as Sawpike, Cucumber fish, Garpike, Green Bone, Sea Clown, Long Nose, Erle, Mackerel Guide, and a smaller variety as the Skipper. Unmistakable with its exceptionally long nose, it grows up to 3ft, and could be said almost to resemble a minature swordfish. It is a member of the flying fish family.

Common to all British coasts, and more so in the south, in late April they precede the mackerel coming inshore by a few weeks and like to roam alone rather than in shoals. They are capable of great speed and can often be seen in play leaping about on the surface like acrobats. In a feeding mood, they are quite voracious, so few baits will be refused.

The lightest tackle will ensure good sport, and where there are mackerel there are likely to be garfish, hunting small mackerel. The usual mackerel spinner is frequently used, or a small float suspending a bait just below the surface. If drift-lining, use live sand-eel and if moving, keep slow for the best results. Prawns and ragworm will be taken, but the bright parts of mackerel or gar skin cut as a thin sliver about 2 by $\frac{1}{2}$in generally prove the most attractive baits.

If a garfish is not hooked at its first rush, it will return again and again, and often becomes foul-hooked. It will not run far when it does take the bait, usually with a rush from below without nibbling or playing with it. When hooked, they will usually leap clear out of the water or skim across the top frantically in all directions. Their bite is not poisonous, neither is the flesh, even though the bones are green.

Gurnard. Half a dozen or so varieties of this species are to be found in British waters, but only three of these are likely to be caught on rod and line.

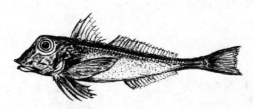

All have large, square-shaped heads protected by bony plates and spines, with a body tapering noticeably towards the tail. Each has two dorsals, the leading edge of which is sharply spined, and also an adequate pectoral by which it can churn up sand and grit to find its sustenance, assisted by six strong feelers under the gills.

The Red Gurnard has triangular scales along the lateral line. The Grey Gurnard is slate grey in colour, often with white spots, and has spiny points along the lateral. One of the smallest types, it seldom grows to larger than 18in.

The Yellow, Sappharine, or Tub Gurnard has an orange hue, with bright blue edging to the large pectorals. Often appearing more red than yellow in colour, it has no triangular scales on the lateral line, nor spines to its dorsals. Other types are the Armed, or Mailed; Streaked; and Shining.

The first three mentioned are fairly common on broken ground in the deeper water around British shores, the Red particularly so in the south. They are not large fish in general but can reach weights of up to 5lb. They are mainly bottom feeders, but do sometimes gather in shoals near the surface and have been hooked at all depths. For baits, they will take worms, fish strips, and some shellfish on the bottom.

Though gurnard themselves make excellent baits when cut up into fish strips for others, they are not usually specially sought after, neither do they offer much in the way of sport. Properly cooked, however, they are said to be very good eating, the Red being the best.

Haddock. This popular fish has a grey-brownish, bronze-like back, which gradually shades out to a white under belly. A black blotch 'thumbprint' is evident on each pectoral fin, together with a blackish lateral line, and there is a small barbel under the chin.

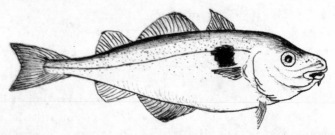

Haddock are fairly abundant, especially around the north and east coasts, but are seldom found in southern waters. Though they have been much overfished, they are still plentiful, some seasons being better than others. Generally speaking, where there is one there are many.

Haddock keep to the deeper waters in the summer months, but begin to approach the coast in the autumn, and during the winter months come closer in, often within range of a dinghy. The best times are from October to March. The average-sized fish is from 2lb to 3lb; a good one is over 5lb and they can even reach double figures.

Bottom feeders, they are usually found over mud or sandy bottoms, and their diet consists of molluscs, crustacea and worms. Legering is the preferred method of catching them, although deep-sea anglers over the deep-water marks use paternosters; so try out both methods. The best baits are lugworm, mussel, squid, or fish strips, and it is necessary to so weight your tackle as to ensure that the bait remains on the bottom.

John Dory. This ugly, sad-looking fish is of peculiar shape, with a large head and mouth, and a smooth body covered with small scales. On each side of the body there is a large brownish-black spot, surrounded by a yellow gold ring. The olive brown body has some yellow bands running along it; when captured and taken from the water, these soon fade out into the surrounding body colour. The front spines of the dorsal and anal fins are often needle sharp and can inflict nasty wounds.

In general a southern waters fish, they frequent rocky coastlines and are believed to spawn in the Channel areas. A fairly slow mover, the John Dory captures its meals by pouting out its mouth and sucking in its prey with its 'jet stream'; anything within a foot radius is drawn into the concertina-shaped folding mouth and quickly enclosed.

Driftlining with light gear offers good sport, with a spiral added if the tide is strong. Float fishing from rocks over and around any seaweed beds may also take them, letting the float roam with the bait swimming near midwater. Do not fish too deep in very hot weather.

Live sand-eels are ideal baits, and they will be attracted by any kind of fish bait, but immediately they discover that there are strings attached to a bait, they will expel it fast. They seldom take a dead bait and will often be found near the surface in hot weather, searching for brit.

Lamprey, Ling, and *Lumpsucker*. These three species may possibly come your way some time and are not easy of recognition. They are therefore included in their alphabetical order, though two are neither interesting nor attractive.

The Lamprey: The (Greater Spotted) Sea Lamprey is a long, eel-like creature, dark greenish brown in colour and mottled with black spots. Fully grown, it can run to about 3ft in length.

It has no true mouth, or jaw, but in its place there is a huge sucker, fully equipped with horned teeth and a rasping tongue. They should be treated with the utmost caution, and killed off forthwith. Beware especially of that sucker mouth, for it really can take the skin from your hand.

The Ling is a really deep-water fish, so unless your shoreline is such an area, or there is a wreck close inshore, you are unlikely to meet one. Unlike the lamprey and lumpsucker, ling

will provide good sport and are usually found in conger areas over rocky terrain, where they will attack any type of fish bait. Average weight is round 15lb, and length 3 to 5ft.

The Lumpsucker is another ugly, though rather more gaudy creature, that you might possibly capture on one of your fishing

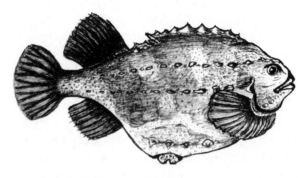

outings, and which can be readily identified from the accompanying illustration. The disc-like sucker is at the base, whilst the body is of a yellowish colour. Note, too, the rough, lumpy topsides.

Mackerel. This highly streamlined and fast-swimming fish is bright blue-green in colour, with irridescent wavy bands on its back, and a small number of regular patterned fins before the tail, which are termed finlets.

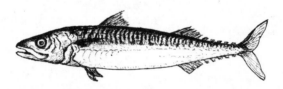

Mackerel are continuous roamers, going wherever their food may be and cannot be relied upon to make regular appearances at specific localities. They arrive from deep water about May, and remain in inshore waters until September. They first appear in small shoals, which meet and congregate into larger ones until by August the shoals may contain thousands of such fish, always on the move.

In the later months, storms and the cooler water will gradually cause the shoals to break up and they will begin to move away in search of deeper water. By December, there are only a few to be found individually cruising around on the bottom.

Details of the many and varied methods of catching them were described on p. 116 and they will not be choosey about baits, providing they have both flash and movement. In addition to fish strips, worms, or squid, all types of artificials, feather lures, bright spoons, rubber eels and spinners will be found useful. Flapping ragworms are best when using a float and the rod should be kept working up and down now and again to flutter the bait.

Mackerel feed at varying depths, ranging from the surface to many fathoms down, and the shoals keep pretty well to fish of much the same size. Rainy weather and strong winds tend to keep them well below surface.

Monkfish. So called for its appearance of wearing a cowl, the monkfish is actually a member of the shark family, though it looks somewhat like a skate whose wings have been compressed. Its proper name is Angel Fish, but it is also called Angel Ray, and, because of its shape, Fiddle Fish.

It has a flattened head and body with broad wing-like pectorals that are not attached to the head. In colour, it is brown to grey above, with both light and dark splotches and spots, and wide spiracles set well back behind the eyes.

Monkfish may be found all round the British coast, but are most plentiful around the south-west and in the Channel area. They appear from deep water in the spring as the water gets warmer, and often return regularly to the same haunts each year, where they remain until the late autumn change of temperature.

Bottom feeders, they are usually taken over sand, mud, or a similar mixed bottom area, and are liable to be caught on whatever tackle or by any method you happen to be using. As they prey on other fish, they are particularly likely to be attracted by a large fish bait and may sometimes be taken from a beach, though in most cases they are caught just by chance.

Mullet. There are three distinct species to be found, all somewhat similar with thick bodies, short broad heads and small mouths. They are silvery in appearance with dark, lengthwise stripes which transform the regular pattern of diamond-shaped scales into small triangles; the top of the body is dark, decreasing to a light belly.

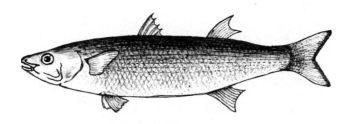

The Grey Mullet, as illustrated, is the most common, being the 'thick lip' variety. It is bluish-grey in colour and has scales on its rear dorsal and anal fins. These fish usually weigh from 2 to 5lb, but can reach double figures.

The Red Mullet is the 'thin lipped' variety. Compared with the grey, the scales are missing, and the distance between the dorsals is much less.

The Golden-grey Mullet is the least common of the three; it has a gold spot on the gills and a smaller one behind the eyes. It can attain a weight of up to 6lb.

Shoals will appear first in April, and frequently haunt harbours, estuaries, docks, or any brackish waters, staying until October. They are particularly plentiful during summer and autumn in the Irish Sea and Channel areas.

In the summer, mullet are usually surface feeders, or may be found nudging amongst weeds at any depth. Their food consists mainly of shrimps, worms, and molluscs and they settle down on the bottom at night. They generally enter harbours on the early flood flow, and if the water is not too disturbed they will often come inshore in search of the microscopic marine life abounding on piers, piles and moorings. They are more difficult to catch in harbours than off shore, and the special tackle called for is described on p. 117.

Plaice. A most popular fish and excellent food value, plaice in general are much larger than the flounder or the dab. They grow fairly slowly, so if you hook an immature fish, unhook it carefully and return it to the sea to help conserve our dwindling stock.

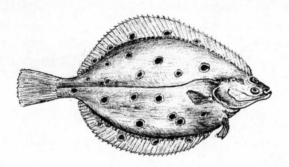

Plaice are brown on top, with well defined red or orange spots, and a clear white underbelly. There is great variety in the pattern of the spots, some being almost invisible, whilst others are ringed. The eyes are on the right, and behind them is a hard knobbly protuberance.

They may be found in most non-rocky areas and usually arrive inshore about the end of April, seeking out the hard sand, shingle, or mud areas. They are usually gone by the end of November, but may still be caught in deep waters.

Plaice will travel considerable distances to obtain their food, seldom staying very long in one location and moving on with the incoming tide. Their staple diet is worms and shellfish, but they go off the feed completely when dusk sets in, hence very few are taken at night. They often keep to about 1ft off bottom, so that a pater is a good choice of tackle.

The best bait without doubt is lugworm, but they are partial to all the usual offerings, even a piece of conger, but for large ones a quarter or even a half herring should be tried. Local baits are best. Bites are a well defined series of quick nibbles. On feeling these, draw off a little line, then tauten up and reel in a little, hoping for the best.

Plaice will remain alive for many hours out of water, and when handling them the sharp spine on the ventral fin should be avoided.

Pollack and ***Coalfish.*** Both of the same family, these two are listed together to faciliate recognition of their individual differences.

The Pollack has a bronze-like, dark green back and a silvery white belly. A gold lateral line curves upwards over the pectoral fin, and it has a noticeable protruding under-jaw but no barbel.

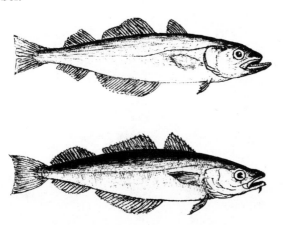

Comparative details of pollack (above) and coalfish

The Coalfish has a blue-green, almost black back and a clear white belly. The lateral line is practically straight with no traces of gold. The jaws are level, without protrusions and it has a small barbel under the lower jaw.

141

The small fish of both species are called Billet, Cuddy, or Nag, while mature pollack are known as Laithe, Leet or Skeet; the mature coalfish is called Saithe.

Pollack are more abundant in the south, and coalfish in the north, their favourite locations being rocky coasts and weedy shores. They tend to surface at dawn and dusk, but go deeper in daylight. They feed at all depths, and often lay in wait for the tide to bring food. A sliding pater could locate them, but they lose interest at slack water.

Legering is not often successful, but driftlining will often pay off. Whichever method is used, it is important to keep the bait moving, remembering that pollack will often follow the bait when retrieving and are capable of a late grab. Baits are of the general type and bites are unmistakeable. A downward rush may follow; so if the water is deep give him his head before checking him.

Pouting. A prolific species that abounds everywhere, pouting are also called Pout, Whiting Pout, Bib, Brassy, and many other names.

It has a short body, giving a deep, pot-bellied appearance, and has a barbel on its lower jaw. It is of a coppery colour, and some have vertical broad dark stripes superimposed, and a dark spot on the pectoral. The average weight is from 1 to 3lb, but it can reach 5lb.

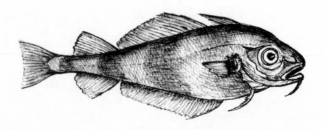

Pouting can be found in most places and favour a habitat of rocks and weeds. The bigger ones are found in deeper waters, or mingling with the whiting shoals. Their season in British waters is from October to May and, being prevalent round all shores and in harbours round walls and piles, they are likely to be included in any day's catch.

As they are bottom feeders, a leger and paternoster is most useful, light tackle being preferable, but if in a rocky area where a cod or other heavy species could abound, do not fish too fine.

Hermit tail, worms, crab, limpet, or any rock-haunting fish make good baits and though small hooks are to be preferred, they are not essential as pouting will generally commit suicide whenever they see a baited hook. They will even take shelled garden snails.

A small pouting of under 4oz is an ideal bait to swim for enticing a conger. They quickly die when taken from the water but can be used as conger bait whether alive or dead.

Rays. Generally classified with skates, there are many varieties of this species to be found in British waters and the following are some that could be encountered. Recommended baits, fishing methods, and information as to their habits will be found on p. 121.

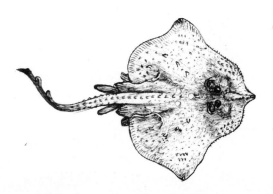

The Thornback Ray (illustrated) is the commonest and comes further inshore than is often realised. It has an upper surface disc of brown with marbled spots, each being bordered by darker spots or rings, and scattered without pattern all over. Four rows of hooked spines adorn each wing, with others on tail and snout. Those taken from a boat off shore usually average about 10lb.

The Sting Ray, round shaped and dark in colour, is easily distinguishable by its whip-like tail, middled by a serrated spine which it will lash about with abandon, so treat it with the utmost caution.

The Blonde Ray is a light fawn colour on top and has small dark spots extending to the margin of the heart-shaped disc. It also has about a dozen pale symmetrical patches on each side of its wings. The underside of the disc margins carry a border of small spines. It can reach the 25lb mark, and a length of about 3½ft.

The Spotted Ray varies in colour, but is mostly dark brown. The upper surface may or may not be spotted, but if so the spots are round and of darker colouring. It has a shortish snout, and some sharp spines on its back.

The Sandy Ray is reddish-grey to dark brown, on top, though some may be light brown. Creamy yellow spots, bordered with brown, pattern the disc.

The Cuckoo Ray, ranging in length up to about 2½ft, has a heart-shaped disc, and on its wings are eye-like spots of dark dots ringed with yellow borders.

The Painted Ray has a grey top blotched with brown and white. Average length is 2 to 3ft.

The Undulated Ray is quite unmistakeable, with its tiger-like markings.

Scad. Not to be confused with the Shad, this fish is commonly known as the Horse Mackerel, and sometimes as a Scousher.

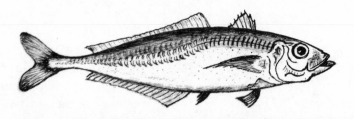

Its back is a dark olive green, with some blue tinges, while the underside is lighter, shading out to greenish blue and faint gold. It has a pronounced lateral line which is covered with bony plates set in a herring-bone pattern, and is thus easily recognisable. There may be a large dark spot on the gill covers, though this is not always present. The main colouration shows up well when first caught, but quickly fades.

Distribution is varied, but scad usually precede the mackerel shoals, arriving in early summer around the south-west coasts in large shoals and then spreading out to reach the Irish Sea on one side, and the Wash on the other.

Surface-living fish, they have a preference for rocky reefs, groynes, piers, and any weed-covered areas. The best time to try for them is after dark, when they rise in huge shoals; thundery weather, too, will bring them up any time.

Most methods will take them but the ideal tackle is a small sliding float with a 6ft trace and a size 6 hook. They average 1½lb during the summer. All the usual baits are accepted, and as they are cannibal fish they will readily take a fish strip of their own kind. They also make very good bait for other species.

Scad will often oblige when other fish are off their feed or playing hard to get. It is a reasonably sporting fish, boring down to the rocks being a favourite tactic, and they can be attracted by illumination at night. When handling scad take care to avoid injury from the spine before the dorsal.

Shad. A member of the herring family, and comparatively rare, there are two distinct species, the Allis Shad and Twaite Shad.

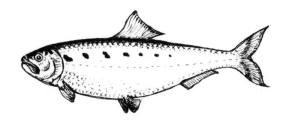

The Allis is the larger of the two, often attaining a weight of 8lb and growing to 2ft in length. They look somewhat like a cross between a plump bass and a herring, and the body is silvery with a blue, rainbow sheen. The lower jaw fits into a hollow in the upper one. The Twaite is somewhat similar, and distinguishable by a line of large spots evenly spaced along the top of its sides (see illustration), whereas the Allis has but one spot. The Twaite Shad rarely exceeds 3lb.

The Allis runs in during late April, and the Twaite follows in May, entering the estuaries and ascending to the upper reaches of many freshwater outlets, continuing to arrive through June. During this spawning season they can be heard rushing and swishing through the waters, and on completion the spent fish return to the sea. Even then, they do not wander far from the shore until the cold weather returns, usually remaining close to the river they have ascended.

Although rarely taken at sea, they are much more widespread than is often thought to be the case, and the angler will usually catch them when he is spinning with a spoon, especially if it is a fly-spoon, or infrequently when float fishing for mullet.

They are said to be decreasing in numbers, apparently driven away by the state of pollution in some of the rivers. They are not especially fished for, and from a culinary standpoint are deemed coarse and unappetising.

Skate. These fish, similar to the Rays, are flat members of the shark family, being cartilagenous (ie, having no bones). They are not referred to as flatfish by anglers, who reserve this description for those species compressed laterally during their metamorphosis when young, ie turbot, plaice, etc, whereas in the skate family the compression of the body is vertical. Note also that the terms 'Skate' and 'Ray' have now become synonymous (as is frequently exemplified by reference to a 'Thornback Skate').

There are but three named skate types in British waters and though shore and harbour anglers are most unlikely to encounter them, very occasional visitors do sometimes arrive.

The Common, or Grey Skate, is by far the largest found round the coast, and in deep waters these heavyweights,may run as high as 100lb. It is grey in colour, tinged to a purple brown, with a patchy light grey pattern of irregular splotches, whilst the underside is a blueish white.

The White Skate is a separate but similar species to the Grey except that the under surface is clear white with no trace of blue.

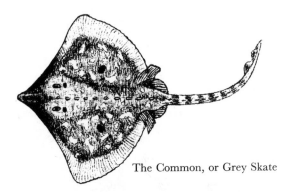

The Common, or Grey Skate

The Flapper Skate has a brownish upper surface, whilst the under belly is white with an irregular pattern of black spots. It has a slightly elongated snout, and grows to around 2ft. This species is not common anywhere in British waters, but it could possibly be encountered.

Apart from the Long-nosed Skate, a real voracious fish-eater and a denizen of the deep, other so-called or named skates are classified as rays. For habits and fishing methods, see p. 121.

Sole. There are more than half a dozen different varieties of this species, all mostly oval in shape.

The Common Sole is grey or brownish in colour, with a large black spot on the pectoral, which itself is large. The mouth is below the snout, the lower nostril being the larger.

The Sand Sole has brown blotches or black spots on the body, and a black spot on the pectoral. The underside is white, the mouth is below the snout, and the lower nostril is the larger.

The Lemon Sole has a smaller head than the other two and its mouth is at the end of its snout. Some dark patches appear on the regular oval-shaped body, and the lateral line is straight.

The Variegated, or Thick-back Sole, is more of a reddish brown, with six or seven dark cross bands extending to black at the fins. The mouth is at the end of the snout, pectorals are small, and there are some smooth scales on the body.

147

The Solenette is a very small variety up to 5in, with small pectorals and no bands.

Soles can be found inshore almost throughout the year, but move into deep water to spawn in the spring, when they are away, some at a time, for about five weeks. They haunt mud or sand areas, soft ground, the piles around piers, and often the gullies running between clumps of rock.

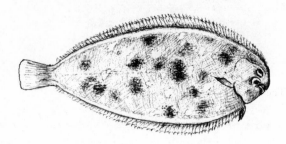

They feed mainly at night and though warm, calm weather will bring them nearer the shore, there is small chance of taking them near heavy surf; a long, low ripple is the ideal.

A 2in worm, razor fish and all the usual baits are most effective on the bottom and use small traces and small hooks to assemble light leger tackle. The bite is a thump but do not strike as they have small mouths.

Tope. Often referred to as the Poor Man's Shark, the tope is also known as the Miller Dog, Penny Dog, and the Shark Dog. Tope fishing is a specialised sport usually carried out in deep waters, but as they have very occasionally been caught from the shore and could get close enough in at some locations, they are included in our list.

In size, tope fill the halfway stage between a dogfish and shark, and while fish around 25lb are common, the record is over 70lb. Brownish grey in top colour, they have a white belly, and a deep notch lower tail lobe.

Distribution is fairly widespread in both summer and winter, and as the water gets warmer, the females come close inshore to bear their young, often 40 to 50 at a time. They become sparse once winter approaches.

Fish-eaters, tope seek out whiting and flatfish as a diet and when hooked will set off at a terrific pace, often doubling back. Many techniques for catching them have been devised, most of them involving a lively outfit, including a quick recovery reel full of strong line, and wire traces to large hooks to counter their fearsome teeth.

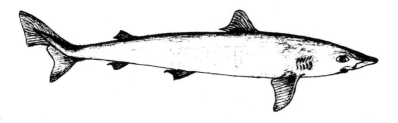

A fresh pout or mackerel, whole, makes an ideal bait, but herring or other large fish fillets are also acceptable. Use a smaller bait if driftlining at anchor, or float fishing, the best being a fish head trailing its internals. Whole fish should be presented to be swallowed head first, with a single hook, size 1 or larger, protruding under the belly. If using two hooks, arrange a size 6 from the gills and a size 4 projecting halfway down the opposite side, binding both snoods at the tail.

Turbot. The largest species of the angler's flatfishes likely to be caught by rod and line, a turbot is a much-prized catch and a great delicacy. It is a broad and roughly diamond-shaped fish by comparison with the brill, which is an ovaloid. It is also scaleless, whereas the brill is smooth scaled on both sides. The top is brownish coloured, with some dark spots on it here and there, and it also has some hard tubercules, like pimples, but not to any set pattern. It has a large mouth, a white underside and the eyes are on the left.

Distribution is general, but these fish are mostly found in fairly deep water—at an average depth of 15 fathoms, but seldom over 25 fathoms.

They are generally to be found where there is a fast run of the tide, and prefer a habitat of sand and gravel banks, lurking along the edges and gullies out of the tidal force awaiting any prey that may come along. April to June sees them settling in, and in the summer months they are at their best, some attaining weights of over 20lb.

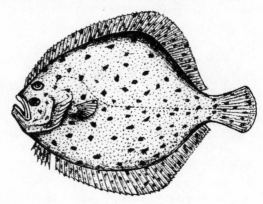

The best way to catch them is by using a long flowing trace, either fished as a leger, or drifting, with strips of fish or small whole ones. In view of the weights they can attain, it is necessary to use strong tackle, but wire traces are not needed. The ideal baits to present to them are small fish in the form of sand-eel, sprats, or any fresh fish cuttings. Once hooked they will actively resist arrest.

Turbot often come close inshore after a storm and may be taken from a deep-water jetty, but they rarely come close in near a beach.

Weever. Generally known as Sting-Fish, and for good reason, the Lesser Weever when fully grown will measure 5 to 7in and will be found in sandy shallows. The Greater Weever (illustrated) runs up to 18in, is the more virulent of the two and swims fairly deep.

The cleft of the mouth points obliquely upwards and this characteristic, together with the highly placed eyes, facilitates identification. The Greater Weever has a light, brownish-yellow body with dark oblique markings on the sides, whilst the Lesser has a greyer-brown back and paler belly, and its first dorsal is black. Watch out for the dark and light streaks on the tail, as these fish can easily be mistaken for gurnards, but most of all note the venomous spines which form the first dorsal, *and* the protruding one on each side of the gill cover. *Do remember them,* for these are highly poisonous and scratches could prove fatal.

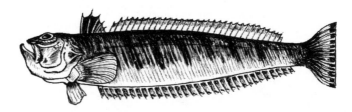

Weevers frequent sandy shallows close inshore where they lie buried in the sand, but sometimes their spines will protrude to become a menace to bathers as well as anglers. They may also be found in rocky pools, as their diet consists mainly of shrimps.

Should you chance to catch one, or perhaps haul one in when a large clump of weed fouls your tackle, do not handle it, but bring it in, pin it down, and with a long-bladed knife, stab or sever the head, cutting off the gill spines and then the first dorsal. Do this before thinking of removing it from the hook, and do not rely on a hand cloth protection as it could be penetrated. Remember, too, that the spines remain poisonous after death.

If pricked by a spine apply a tourniquet above the wound, so that it bleeds and wash continuously in salt water. Later use strong Condy's fluid or a nonsalt solution and seek medical attention. Oddly enough, this fish makes good eating once the dangerous parts have been removed.

Whiting. A member of the cod family, whiting average about 1lb, though a good one may run up to as much as 3lb. They have an all-over silvery appearance, with a dark spot on the roots of the pectoral fin and are well streamlined, with a large mouth and no barbel. They have sharp teeth, so be careful when unhooking as wounds can turn septic.

Distribution is plentiful, and they usually travel in large, dense shoals. They spawn in deep waters in the spring, moving into coastal waters in late autumn and usually staying until February, though they will go earlier if it is really cold.

The best times to catch them are just before and after high water once the tide starts to run, when they will feed voraciously, particularly on a moving bait.

A boat is an advantage as they like deep water—about 8 to 10 fathoms—and are usually found over sandy or grit bottoms. As they are often shoaling from 4 to 6ft up, bottom tackle is not for them, and a pater raised slowly, moved along a bit and dropped again, is a good way to get started. Use a piece of old iron as a killick, on light line, for shifting position, and if you meet a shoal weigh it and trip along easily with them.

Fig. 68   A flasher for whiting

Large hooks are best, snooded by a swivel, and try adorning your hooks with a flasher of silver paper, milk top foil, or yellow sellotape for they will grab this even without bait when on the feed. Use needle sharp hooks as they snatch passing by. Baits can be anything from lug and fish cuts to shellfish, but keep them at the end of the hook so that the fish has to take the hook right into its mouth and is hooked first go. Do not reel in quickly, as often another 'tug and take' may come on the way up. Pier or beach fishing is best at high water ordinary springs and they will feed in the surf when dark.

Wrasse. The most brilliantly coloured of British fish, wrasse are deep in the body with marbled markings, and all have large mouths. There are many sub-species and in some the sexes differ in appearance.

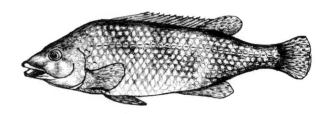

The Ballan Wrasse (illustrated), also called Merrin, or Golden Maid, grows to 16in and weighs up to 5lb. The back and sides are blue green, whilst there are vertical fin markings of orange yellow, and some blue in the scales.

The Cuckoo, or Striped Wrasse is a bright orange red with yellow fins and blue dorsal blotches; the male has some blue body stripes, whilst the female has three black blotches near the tail.

The Corkwing, or Conner Wrasse, is red brown with green and yellow hues and vertical dark brown bands. The lateral line curves downward.

The Scale Rayed and the Rainbow Wrasse are two deep-water species rarely encountered inshore, and there is also a very small type, the Rock Cock Wrasse.

Wrasses are rocky bottom fish and usually haunt the weedy areas, seldom being found on sandy patches; their favourite depth is about 6 fathoms. They may be taken on any bottom tackle, or when float fishing and though they will not run with a bait, they may set course for their refuge if near. The warmer the weather the better their appetite, which they tend to lose as winter approaches.

They posses strong conical teeth, so in addition to the usual worms and fish strips, they will take prawns, peelers, green hardback crabs about the size of a 50p piece, and shellfish. They are not specially fished for but their flesh makes a good general bait for most other species.

Miscellaneous. There are also a few species of small, inedible fish, such as blennies, rock ling, and gobies which may be taken, but they are not sought after and so of little interest to anglers.